The New Teacher of Adults

A Handbook for Teachers of Adult Learners
2nd Edition

by Michael Brady and Allen Lampert

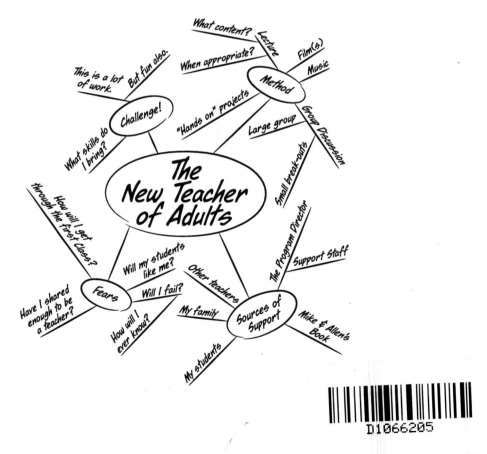

ISBN: 0-9747249-1-2

Published by New Teacher Concepts
Printed by J. Weston Walch Publisher
Copyright 2007 by Michael Brady and Allen Lampert
Original cover and book design by Patrick Corey
www.newteacherconcepts.com

Table of Contents

Acknowledgements

The New Teacher of Adults, its first edition in 2004 and now its second edition, was written with the help of many friends, colleagues, and professional acquaintances with whom we have had the privilege of working over the years. These thoughtful professionals provided us with the generous gift of their time and talents as they offered suggestions, materials, and critical feedback. We wish to thank the following adult education teachers and administrators for reading the manuscript as it was taking shape and for allowing us to use their materials as examples of good teaching practice: Vince Beaulieu, Keith Dawson, Corinne Dellatorre, Barbara Gauvin, Pam Harvey, Victor Caron, Gary Hatch, Larinda Meade, Pam Meader, Jody Meredith, Anne Niemiec, Steve Foss, David Sherman, Judy Storer, Gail Senese and Rob Wood. Julie Cameron, the University of Southern Maine's Executive Director of Marketing and Brand Management, has been an editor and guide. Cathy Emery designed our Web site, newteacherconcepts.com, which has allowed hundreds of educators to find and order our book. Barbara Gauvin originally set this project in motion when she commented that she and her fellow public school adult education directors in Maine could use a good primer on teaching adult learners as a staff development tool.

During the three years between the first and second editions we have been privileged to receive feedback from adult education teachers, both new and experienced, from across the United States and Canada, who have read our book. We have learned from our readers that *The New Teacher of Adults* indeed has been the single-source reference for ideas and tools about teaching that it was our goal to create. We are deeply honored that an audience which began in Maine with public school-based adult educators has spread to community and technical colleges and various other public adult education programs in New Hampshire, Connecticut, New York, Kentucky, Georgia, Louisiana, South Dakota, Arkansas, Texas…in fact all the way to California and its diverse and multi-layered network of adult schools. In fact adult education programs in over 25 states and half the Canadian provinces have used *The New Teacher of Adults.* We hope the new edition of our book will be equally well received.

Michael Brady and Allen Lampert

Preface

The world of adult education, as practiced in public schools (GED/ABE), vocational training, community colleges, corporations, churches, recreation departments, health care institutions, and a wide range of community-based agencies, depends in good measure, on new teachers, many of them part-time. Administrators and program planners often hire as instructors people who are knowledgeable, have technical expertise, are interested in sharing their knowledge, and are highly competent professionals. In other words, people like you. Chances are you feel reasonably confident when thinking about *what* you are going to teach. However, especially if you have not had specific training in the field of education or a range of experiences as a classroom instructor, you may feel significantly less confident about how you will teach.

This point came home to us several years ago (prior to the publication of the first edition) when a respected adult education director in southern Maine, the region where both of us live and work, expressed something of her frustration about this widespread issue. "At the start of each semester I hire new teachers for my program," Barbara said. "They are good, competent professionals. But many of them have never taught adults before. They want me to go over their course plan, help them anticipate problems, and coach them about teaching, but I'm awfully busy trying to run my program and can't always make the time to do this. I wish I could get some help." This book is explicitly written to address this need.

Admittedly a written survival guide isn't the same as one-on-one coaching. But in the hands of new teachers of adults and, as we have learned from many who have read the first edition, experienced teachers of adults, this book is a helpful navigational tool. From the beginning it has been our intention that *The New Teacher of Adults* indeed be a tool. It is meant for practical use. While at times you will read brief sections where we share important theories about adult learning and teaching, our purpose is to provide a wider context so the teaching practice aspects of this book will be understood in more depth and in the end make greater sense.

An aspect of this book we feel is especially important are the numerous examples we offer from our own teaching practices and those of colleagues with whom we have consulted. Within these pages you will find samples of syllabi, advance-organizers, mind-maps, journal entry ideas, evaluation forms, and other instruments which we have found to be useful over the years and which may help you to teach more effectively. While many books have been published on the subject of teaching (written primarily for college-level faculty and often with a strong bent toward theory), we don't know of other current sources in which there these types of practical teaching tools are offered to the reader. We hope this is an especially beneficial characteristic of *The New Teacher of Adults*.

Receiving comments from readers of *The New Teacher of Adults* has been important to us and based on that feedback we have incorporated numerous changes in the second edition. For example, in 2004 we had an entire chapter dedicated to the "Equipped for the Future" standards, an initiative sponsored by the National Institute for Literacy that was all the rage in some states when it was first promulgated in 2000. However a number of educators from widely disparate regions of the United States informed us that "Equipped for the Future" is not used by adult education programs in their state. Therefore we have chosen to delete that chapter. (Note: Readers of the second edition can still read about "Equipped for the Future" by looking up the Sondra Stein—2000 reference in our *Sources for Further Learning* section.). We have added a new chapter about teaching online, the continuous improvement of teaching, and co-teaching models. Additionally we have strengthened and updated some exemplars.

Being bluntly truthful, we confess that we do not believe one person can teach another person to teach. Teaching, like any complicated and challenging activity, must ultimately be learned by practicing it again and again. And then, no matter how many years of experience we have, teaching is never fully "learned" because every semester and every new class of students brings unique situations and challenges. Teachers are constantly faced with learning new practices, experimenting, and sometimes failing. We often overcome these failures and challenges by sharing our experiences with fellow teachers, obtaining feedback, and thus gaining fresh perspective. It would be sheer foolishness—or hubris—for us to suggest that, through these pages or even coaching you in person, we could teach you to become a good teacher. However, we do feel confident that through these pages we can serve as a beacon and a source of support and perhaps even inspiration. We want our book to be a thoughtful and caring companion, a "guide on the side," as you venture forth into this wonderful journey of teaching adults. And more than anything else, we hope you will deeply and passionately cherish the journey.

Chapter 1:
Why Teach?

Typically, the new teacher of adults approaches this adventure with more questions than answers. Am I prepared for the challenge? Am I smart enough? Will my students respect and like me? Will I be helpful to them? Will my weaknesses be apparent—for example, what if I can't answer someone's question? How can I ensure that we get off to a good start? Why am I doing this to begin with?

While this book will help the beginning teacher to explore and answer all of these questions—and others—we shall begin with the last one, "Why am I doing this to begin with?" Or, put simply, "Why teach?"

We will address this important question from the most valued source we have at our disposal—our experience. We are both teachers of adults. Our combined experience totals more than 30 years and has involved a wide range of teaching forums: university and community college classrooms, public school adult education programs, professional workshops, corporate training, community-based discussion seminars, and one-on-one mentoring. Over time you, the new teacher, will be able to answer this question, "Why teach?" in your own words and use your own examples. Here are ours.

We teach in order to learn
Learning is the primary reason why the field of education and the profession of teaching exist. But we are not just talking about learning achieved by those who enroll in courses or seminars as students. We strongly believe that the teacher is "the first learner." No matter how much we already know about our subject prior to stepping into the role of teacher, we will learn substantially more by thinking about this new role, preparing for classes, and working to develop the appropriate readings, questions, and assignments that are designed to enable others to learn. We have heard from colleagues and have experienced ourselves that in many cases, when evaluating the results of a course, we teachers believe we have learned more about the subject we just taught than any of our students. And none of us who have felt this way took

this as a criticism of our teaching ability as much as a compliment to the power of the learning that accompanies teaching! There is an old saying that continues to reflect something of the efficacy of this idea: "If you want to learn something, teach it!" We hope that whatever subject it is you find yourself teaching, you love it enough to want to learn even more about it than your students will.

We teach to make connections

Learning is all about making connections. And so is teaching. How do ideas interrelate? How does this fact link to other ones? In what ways can we take this thread of a detail and another and eventually spin them into a coherent whole of cloth? How do discrete bits of information expand and mutate and eventually grow into knowledge? When, in the act of teaching, we try to help other people make such connections, we invariably multiply and strengthen our own. We understand the relationships between ideas or events more keenly. We appreciate them more. We grow to love and respect our subject—whether it be history, auto mechanics, personal computers, mathematics, watercolor painting, or anything in the vast lexicon of learning—in ways that were not as profound before we tried to teach them to others.

We teach for stimulation

Teaching is exciting! It is invigorating! It gets the heart pounding and blood rushing through one's veins. Many times, late in the day, after a long series of meetings or other appointments have pretty much tired us out, we find renewed zeal when anticipating the fact that we have an evening class of adults to teach. Our minds dance with ideas as we drive to the school building. Sometimes, when we know we have especially interesting units to teach that evening, we are bursting with anticipation even when we are still many miles and minutes away from our classroom. And when the moment arrives when we physically enter the room in which we'll be teaching that evening, we feel another jolt of energy. It seldom, if ever, fails. Teaching is stimulating. One has to be dead not to feel its force of power.

We teach to get rich spiritually!

Well, it's certainly not to get rich financially. With few exceptions, teaching in adult education is not lucrative (those exceptions tend to involve management and technical consultants working with prosperous business clients). Getting paid $10-$15 per hour to teach GED preparation or a personal enrichment course is not going to put a lot of groceries on the family table. But it can and will feed the soul. We have heard for years and continue to hear from part-time teachers, people who hold regular "day jobs," that their one night of teaching adult education is so satisfying to them, and so bountiful to their state of mind and emotion, that they do not care whether or not they are paid an hourly wage. We also realize that most part-time teachers of adults want and need the monetary income they derive from teaching. But the true potential in teaching for generating wealth does not lie in the financial realm. It is someplace quite different and, we believe, more important. In our attempt to help others, we experience something profound and powerful that cannot be easily described, explained, or categorized. As you teach, these experiences will take on their own special meaning to you and will yield new and heretofore uncharted rewards.

We teach for relationships

We have come to learn that, at its very core, teaching is about ways in which human beings relate to one another. The most brilliant lecturer in the world will not evoke much learning—or at least deep learning—if she or he has not reached out beyond the lectern and touched students in a personal manner. The most artful discussion facilitator will not generate much change in people if true connections to students' wants and needs are not made. Adult learners want guides, mentors, and coaches. They want and need somebody to listen to them, to share insights and stories with them, to grow with them. There is little need in the adult education class for yet another efficient machine downloading information (many people will have already experienced quite enough of that during the day). We teach in order to relate to peoples' minds and hearts. Both are required if we are going to do this work well.

We teach to be remembered

We admit that this sounds a little selfish. But then again, wanting to be remembered later in life or after death, even if by only one or two people, is a profoundly human desire. Is there anyone who is satisfied by the thought of being wholly and completely forgotten? Teachers, perhaps more than any other profession, have staying power in peoples' memories. If you asked an adult to name the five most influential people in their life, chances are good that a classroom teacher or mentor will be on the list.

One of us recently had a conversation with a student about this very issue. This 56 year-old woman grew up in a harsh and uncaring family. But she told the story of her fourth grade teacher who supported her emotionally and instilled confidence in her. Recalling this teacher, this adult woman began to cry. The impact made by her fourth grade teacher, so many decades ago, was obviously deep, positive, and lasting.

Good teachers matter and make a difference (and—beware—bad teachers do, too!). And perhaps the greatest reason why teachers make such an impact on human lives and are justifiably remembered is because. . .

We teach to transform
In the end all the learning, connecting, and relating that teachers engage on a continual basis are aimed toward effecting change. Teaching changes human lives. And changed lives mean a changed world. In 21st century American society teachers at all levels are still not paid as well as many professions nor do we garner the esteem and prestige that is granted to our colleagues in other cultures. Nonetheless, teachers are perhaps second only to parents in their power to influence young lives. And teachers of adults may be second only to immediate family members in our ability to influence growth and change at later stages in the life span.

Teaching transforms. It has the potential to influence deep, constitutional, dramatic, at-the-core changes in personal and professional lives. Adult learners who encounter excellent teaching will not walk away from the experience the same as when they entered. We teachers touch lives and, through the alchemy and admittedly mysterious forces of the teaching-learning process, transform them into something more profound, more able, more confident, more human. And this, above all else, is why we teach.

Chapter 2:
The Basic Characteristics of Adult Learners

Working with adult learners is an extremely rewarding and challenging experience. Unlike students in other venues (i.e., primary, secondary, or post secondary schools) adult learners attend school because they want to be there. Also, adults bring a wealth of life and work experiences into the classroom that adds tremendous value to the educational experience for everyone. Here are some basic characteristics of adult learners.

- Adult students are voluntary learners.
- They need a comfortable learning environment.
- Students join adult education programs in reaction to a life-changing event (i.e., retirement, the need to obtain new skills for employment opportunities) or to seek recreational/enrichment activities.
- In general, adults stay on task; but they usually retain knowledge more efficiently in the first several minutes of class, so use your time wisely.
- They come from diverse cultural/social backgrounds.
- Adult students have different levels and styles of learning.
- They are often tired when they come to class.
- Adult learners want some control over their learning experience.
- They will resist being forced, judged, or embarrassed into doing things.

Let's examine these elements in more detail.

Adult students are voluntary learners. Adult learners typically want to be in your classroom and they hate to have their time wasted. They have made a conscious decision to take your course, often with a mixed set of motives. Sometimes they are taking your course to meet program requirements towards a larger goal (GED) or they are taking your course for personal enrichment and enjoyment (gardening). Adult learners will "vote with their feet." If they find value in your class, they stay. If they don't, they often leave and find one that gives them what they need and want.

They need a comfortable learning environment. You want to take the necessary steps to make sure fundamental physical needs are met. (i.e., regular breaks, comfortable seating, good lighting) Furthermore, students want to feel welcome and respected. Getting to know their names as soon as possible is advisable. Often, adults look for learning environments that allow them to work closely with other students, thus providing them with a learning tool with as much informality as possible.

Students join adult education programs in reaction to a life-changing event or to seek recreational/enrichment activities. Students often come to adult education programs because they are looking for additional job training, have recently been laid off, are new arrivals to the United States and need more education, are learning to read, are earning their high school diploma, or are facing retirement. In addition, students seek a learning experience that gives them pleasure and/or personal enrichment in vocations and avocations they always wanted to pursue but never had the time. These classes may include gardening, painting, dance, cooking, language, computers, etc.

In general, adults stay on task; but they usually retain knowledge more efficiently in the first several minutes of class so use your time wisely. Unlike many younger students from public education venues, adults have the capacity to stay focused with their work. However, most adults retain the majority of information disseminated within the first several minutes of class. Therefore, it is critical that you use the opening minutes judiciously and effectively. This is when your students will learn best!

They often come from diverse cultural/social backgrounds. Some of your students may come from different countries. English could be their second, third, or even fourth language. These students bring their own unique perspective about the world into class. If this is your first experience working in these circumstances, we believe you will find it extremely challenging and rewarding. Simple things like how your students maintain (or don't maintain) eye contact, how their body language presents itself and how you, in turn, present yourself may have an impact on your class. Your level of sensitivity to your students' backgrounds will enhance your ability to communicate with them. Be patient with your students. Just as you adjust to them, they need to adjust to you and to their fellow students. Some of our most rewarding teaching experiences have included episodes of watching classes come together from extremely diverse cultural, social, and economic backgrounds.

Adult students have different styles of learning. Adult learners generally learn by visualizing, reading, writing, speaking, listening, and manipulating. (Sonbuchner, 1991) Below is an abbreviated example of statements a student might decide to check off that reflects most accurately their learning style. As students go through the full questionnaire, trends develop concerning their learning preferences. Here are samples of statements that help determine a student's learning style. They include:

Read	I like to read in my spare time.
	I like to read a report or article rather than be told what's in it.
Listen	I like to listen to people discuss things.
	I learn better by listening to a lecture than by taking notes.
Visual	I can remember something by "seeing" it in my mind.
	I remember people's faces better than their names.
Write	I take notes when I read to understand the material better.
	I take lecture notes to help me remember the material.
Speak	I understand the material better when I read it out loud.
	I learn best when I study with other people.
Manipulate	I would rather do experiments than read about them.
	I learn better by handling objects.

(Sonbuchner, 1991)

Recently, adult educators have paid more attention to brain research and its impact on adult learning. Some key factors concerning the brain that may influence how you structure and teach your class include:

- Responds best to new stimuli or content.
- Remembers best the things that happen at the beginning and the end of an event.
- Learns most efficiently in 20-minute segments.
- Determines what will be remembered based on whether it perceives that the information makes sense.
- Is better at remembering material that has strong emotional content.
- Needs to be trained to organize and retrieve information.
- Makes what is practiced permanent, whether it is right or wrong.

Regardless of their learning style, many adults prefer to participate actively in their learning experience. They enjoy small group work that encourages informality, and enjoy learning from their own experiences and the experiences of their peers. Also, they are self-directed learners, taking responsibility for their own learning. Your ability to implement learning experiences that takes advantage of your students' learning styles will help them understand and apply what you are teaching.

They are often tired when they come to class. Many of your students will be coming to your class directly from their work, often rushing with little or no dinner. They will be tired and often irritable. They will certainly appreciate any teaching approaches you can use which provides liveliness, a sense of humor, and different methods of instruction (i.e., group work, change of pace exercises, etc.) From an instructional standpoint, remember that how you handle the first several minutes of your class may determine their ability to retain critical information and important concepts.

Adults want some control over their learning experience. They like to be able to set their own learning goals (when possible) based on their own needs, enjoy the flexibility to sometimes determine what they do and do not need, and like to be free to choose how to use information and feedback. This may not always be possible, but remember, you are working with adult learners. They have more maturity than children and adolescents and have the right to make certain decisions about their learning experiences. Potential factors that will motivate adult learners include:

- Maintaining active involvement (planning, organizing, determining content, and selecting methods of instruction and evaluation).
- Receiving immediate feedback.
- Course relevancy in terms of content, instruction, and the applicability of the material.
- Course content that is designed to meet the student's goals.
- Experiencing small successes towards achieving larger personal and professional goals.

They will resist being forced, judged, or embarrassed. As a teacher, we advise you to suspend harsh or rigidly set preconceptions. Instead, see yourself as an equal learning partner in the classroom. You may find some students may need to "pass" on certain activities (especially in the beginning) that they feel uncomfortable with. Again, be patient, and take it slow. It is critical that you pay close attention to your students' emotional and psychological safety.

We could add other factors for you to consider when working with adult learners, but this list should provide you a good start in understanding your students. In sum, we advise you apply the "golden rule" to your teaching: Treat your students as would like to be treated: with respect, dignity, openness, and a degree of flexibility. As you continue to read this book, additional tools will be presented to aid you in your teaching experience. These tools will give you ways to get to know your students better.

Chapter 3:
Working with "At Risk" Students

When we enter our first classroom as a teacher, we face different types of students from different backgrounds and experiences. Some of your students may have experienced difficult circumstances that have led them into your classroom. While this adds to the pleasure we face as teachers, it also presents unique challenges and concerns.

The *American Heritage Dictionary* (2nd edition) defines "risk" as "a factor, element or course involving uncertain danger, hazard." In what way does this come into play in our conversation about teaching adults?

Frequently, we teach adults who have not had positive educational experiences. This is frequently seen in GED, high school completion, or even job training classes. Adults often come back to school bringing with them a lifetime of negative educational experiences. They may have dropped out in high school and left school under difficult circumstances. They may see themselves as not having the ability to learn, they may lack confidence, and they may not be comfortable accepting compliments. These students can be suspicious of authority in the classroom, and they may be fearful of being asked questions they have no answers to, thereby being seen as dumb by their peers or the teacher. One consistent factor for these students is the fear they feel coming back to school and questioning whether they will even stick it out. Furthermore, they often come from unstable homes involving a myriad of personal difficulties (i.e., physical abuse, emotional abuse, drug or alcohol dependency).

The term "at risk" may also apply to students who are new to the United States. They can be fearful of what they may face in your classroom. They may come from countries having experienced personal horrors many of us cannot imagine (loss of loved ones, starvation, war, even torture). In addition, these students often bear the additional pressure of trying to learn a new language to survive in their new country.

Your ability to work with students who have these feelings and experiences will present unique challenges to you. Both authors have taught thousands of hours and we are still learning new teaching techniques and approaches in working with students at risk. We have no one answer we can share with you, but here are some ideas you can keep in mind.

- Set clear expectations. Students from challenging backgrounds sometimes struggle with making decisions about their learning. Keep goals and assignments clear and specific, especially in the beginning.
- React, but don't overreact. Stay calm in handling the events swirling around in your classroom. Don't be afraid to respond to what is happening, but some students may try to "test" you. Your ability to stay calm may increase their willingness to stay. Don't give students an easy excuse to give up.
- Never use a red marker or pen when writing on papers or tests. Red is a color many students associate with failure. Use green, blue, or purple—anything but red!
- Develop a "failure proof" exercise to start your class. The initial minutes of your first class will be critical to building confidence for students who are uncomfortable being there.
- Ask your local administrator if there are former students from the adult education program who have received their GED (or other type of certificate) from the district in which you are teaching. Inviting them to come in and talk about their experiences as a student will have a positive and lasting impact on the students in your classroom. Students listen to other students! They can serve as effective and powerful role models.
- Mix your teaching approaches to make sure that all learning styles are being addressed. For example, create situations where you discuss concepts (allowing some students to take notes) followed with handouts. This gives everyone in class a chance to take advantage of their learning style.
- At risk students generally perform better in well-structured learning environments; predictability helps. These individuals like to know what is coming on a class-by-class basis.
- Use methods of self-evaluation so students can gauge their own progress. We recommend the use of brief reflection papers that students can quickly create and that help to show direct and immediate accom-

plishments. Don't hinge everything on "big" tests.

- In time, try to find out why a student has dropped out in his or her prior schooling. The information may be very useful in helping you devise strategies to keep him or her in class.

- Develop a strategy for contacting students who stop attending class. We recommend calling them after their first absence. Waiting longer often gives the student the wrong impression that they can set their own attendance rules, or worse, that there is no reason to continue. When possible, call absent students and encourage them to come back to class. This effort also communicates that you care about them and want them to succeed.

- Be prepared to be flexible. While this may seem to contradict our earlier comment setting clear and specific goals and assignments, at risk students often come to class with unique sets of problems. While you want to set clear expectations, be ready to be flexible in working with them.

At risk students will often make up a portion of your class. While they can create frustrating situations for you to contend with, they will also present highly rewarding results. When at risk students have been asked what things are important to them in adult education teachers, they have mentioned several key qualities. These include:

- Be consistent in approach and policy
- Maintain an atmosphere of fairness
- Give honest and direct feedback, but don't punish or demean
- Listen to your students
- Be firm, yet patient
- Check-in with students as the class progresses and see how things are going

When adult educators follow these simple suggestions, all students benefit. At risk students are taking your class for many of the same reasons as everyone else. They want to improve their lives and/or find enjoyment in an environment that has not always given them a positive experience. The type of learning environment you create will go a long way toward making sure everyone in class has a meaningful and productive learning experience.

Chapter 4:
Planning a New Class and Building a Syllabus

How do you plan to teach a class and create a syllabus? This chapter is designed to assist you in planning your course and creating a syllabus.

According to The *American Heritage Dictionary* (2nd Edition), the definition of a syllabus is "an outline or brief statement of the main points of a test, lecture, or course of study." There are different styles of syllabi. Later in this chapter we will provide you with several examples. Some adult educators prefer to split the concepts of a course outline and a syllabus into different categories and present them in different formats. In general, a course outline presents a schedule when various course content and material will be taught. The syllabus, in contrast, focuses on course objectives, requirements, general course information, and methods of evaluation. Furthermore, the syllabus can be considered a "contract" between you and your students. It establishes the grading parameters, how you will assess students' performance. Many adult educators use the course syllabus to present course objectives/requirements as well as a comprehensive outline/schedule of their course.

However, prior to creating a syllabus, you must have a clear idea of what you will be teaching. This involves a bit of planning on your part. Here are some key questions you will want to consider prior to creating your syllabus. These questions can be asked if you are planning to teach an existing course or if you are creating a new one.

- Why would people want to take this class?
- What information do you want to share with students? Why that information and not something else?
- What are your goals? (You may want to create both a course overview and specific objectives for each class section)
- How will students change by way of the course? What new skills, knowledge, or attitudes are anticipated?
- How will you assess student learning?

There are questions that you will need to consider if you are creating a brand new course. In fact, the adult education director will be taking these questions into account as well, but it does no harm having you think about these issues. These questions include:

- How much time will I need to teach the course?
- What are the potential costs? (books/supplies, labs, equipment needed)?
- How is this course different than others that are currently offered?

Often, an adult education director will ask you to prepare a proposal to teach a new course. They may have a form for you to complete that will contain most of the above factors stated above. Directors will also be able to help determine potential costs associated with the course.

Once you have carefully considered your answers to the above questions, you can create a syllabus. We strongly recommend you first ask for a current syllabus from your program director if you are teaching a course that has already been taught. In fact, it has been our experience that the director will probably offer it to you as a matter of course. As a first time teacher, we suggest you accept all the resources offered you. In general, following the format of a prior teacher may be the most prudent strategy to begin with, unless the director asks you not to use the existing material. You can always make changes to the original syllabus given you based on your observations as the course progresses. Generally, we all make changes to colleagues' syllabi to get us started. We have our own style and ideas, and it only takes one semester of using someone else's material before we make changes to meet our needs. However, if you need to create a new syllabus right away, here are some key points that you may want to include:

- The name of the course
- Your name, e-mail address (if possible), phone number to school
- Description of course
- Objectives of course
- Administrative matters (grading criteria, attendance policy, etc.)
- Required books/materials
- Course outline/schedule (description of assignments/projects)
- Evaluations

Of course, there are many different ways to handle the creation of your syllabus. The type of course you are teaching and the ways you decide to communicate various elements of course content will affect how your syllabus looks. In addition, we suggest you talk to your students on the first night of class about the syllabus. Go over it with them. Find out if there are things that you may have left out.

There are a variety of styles you can use as a guide when you create your syllabus, but you need to create one that meets the needs of your students. Some syllabi should be more detailed than others.

Here are a few examples:

Exhibit 4-1

**Syllabus Example
Traditional Model**

(This approach includes a full syllabus and course outline)

COMPUTER LITERACY FOR BEGINNERS

Instructor: Daniel Abonte
Home Phone: (207) 780-5312
E-Mail: dalbonte21457@aol.com

Course Hours: Monday & Wednesday 6:00-9:00 p.m.
Location: Lewiston Adult Education Room #250
Class starts on January 2 and ends February 22, 2006

Course textbook and materials: *Learning Computers* by Stephen Karl

Course Prerequisites & Description:

No computer or typing experience is necessary. This beginner course teaches you the basics and gives you the confidence to enjoy working with your computer. In addition, you will learn about equipment and terminology. You will also get hands-on experience in our classroom using Windows, word processing, database, spreadsheet, and other software packages. This course provides a good foundation necessary for anyone seeking to use computers on a regular basis or planning a future education in the computer field.

Course Specifications:

1. Total hours scheduled for in-class instruction   45
2. Estimated hours required for home work   10
3. Estimated hours of total student effort   55 Hours

Diploma or certificate credit   1

Course Objectives:

Upon successful completion of this course, the individual should be able to:

1. Recognize and use basic computer terminology.
2. Recognize and utilize PC hardware devices.
3. Understand and describe the purpose of primary and secondary data storage.
4. Organize data and perform proper directory structure.
5. Distinguish between system software and application software.
6. Demonstrate a working knowledge of word processing, spreadsheet, and database software.
7. Utilize the Internet to acquire information and research.
8. Incorporate the knowledge acquired from this course for use in home, at work, and future education courses.

Course Requirements:

Attendance of all scheduled classes is mandatory. Student will be required to participate in the learning process, and all in-class assignments must be completed. All quizzes and the final exam must be completed.

Should a student not be able to attend a scheduled class, the student will be required to complete a make-up assignment. Any missed assignment is due by the following class. Any assignment not turned in will forfeit points and student will be considered absent for that class. It will be the student's responsibility to arrange with the instructor to make up all missed quizzes and exams. Any make-up classes or exams done during regularly scheduled classes will not be accepted.

Should a student be absent for more that two classes, that student must receive permission from the Adult Education Director to complete and receive credit for the course providing the student completes all make-up assignments and requirements.

Grading:

| Class participation | 80% |
| Exams and quizzes | 20% |

Course Outline and Content

Week 1:

Orientation and Class Introductions

Terms and buzzwords
Explanation of hardware and software
RAM and ROM
What are bits, bytes, kilobytes, and gigabytes
What's on your keyboard and getting friendly with the mouse
Turning on your computer properly
Signing on to the network and server
Getting on to the network server
Getting around on the Windows desktop
Shutting down the computer properly

Using software and storage devices

    Disks and hard drives
    Proper handling and storage of diskettes
    The parts of the diskette
    How to format a diskette
    Inserting and removing the diskette
    Creating directories and sub-directories
    Using word processing software
    Typing my first paragraph
    Saving my first paragraph
    Getting around the paragraph and editing those typos
    Save that edited text

Week 2:

More word processing and storing files

    Quick review of previous week
    Retrieving that file
    Centering, bolding, underlining, and fonts
    More editing with word processing and let's see those hidden characters
    How to use spell check
    Let's print a document
    Word processing's global search and replace exercise

Word processing getting a little deeper

    Review prior class
    How and when to copy and paste
    How and when to cut and paste
    What is clipboard and how it works
    In-class project

Week 3:

Introducing Spreadsheets

      What are spreadsheets?
      Explanation of rows, columns, cells
      Label data and value data cells
      Emphasize cell reference
      What is range of cells?
      Working with simple formulas and SUM functions
      Create a simple budget
      Saving your budget spreadsheet

Spreadsheet formulas, functions, and formatting

      Review prior class material
      Retrieve and adding to the budget spreadsheet
      Adding AVG, MIN, MAX functions to the budget sheet
      When to use fill-in right and fill-down
      How to format the spreadsheet
      Saving and printing the spreadsheet

Week 4:

Wrapping up spreadsheets

      More formatting the worksheet
      When to use absolute cell referencing
      Graphs and charts in spreadsheets
      Create a check register spreadsheet
      Taking a look at other pre-designed spreadsheets and what they do

Computers and components

      Discussion on types of computers
      What to look for when buying a computer

Components and compatibility
Using your computer check list
Hands-on opening the computer (let's see what's inside)

Week 5:

Working with Databases

What is a database?
Explanation of field names, records and forms
Create your first address database form
Entering the data
Saving the records

More Database

Editing and deleting records
Creating a database report
Printing the database report
Creating queries in a database
Making reports from queries

Week 6:

Putting it all together

Review of word processing, spreadsheets, and database
Using that spreadsheet data in a word processing document
Using that database address file for mail merge in word processing
Adding graphics to word processing documents and spreadsheets
Saving and printing our work

Creating a special project

Design project based on instructor guidelines.

Week 7:

Using the Internet

> Modem types and speeds
> What is the World Wide Web?
> Explanation of types of providers and fees
> What does logging on to a provider mean?
> Using browsers and search engines
> E-mail

Review

> Review of word processing using other software and computers
> Review of spreadsheets and database using other software and computers
> A word about other operating systems

Week 8:

Final class meeting

> Taking a look at what we covered
> Where to go from here
> Discussing education requirements and opportunities
> Discussing job requirements and opportunities
> Grades and good luck to everyone!

Exhibit 4-1 follows the more traditional format that educators use when conveying course information to their students. We deliberately used a common course taught in almost all adult education districts (i.e., computers) for this traditional format. Course objectives, information, requirements, structure, grading, and a full class schedule and outline are presented. This type of syllabus is often used for academic courses. However, there are other models you can use.

Exhibit 4-2 is a variation of the traditional approach. While it includes much of the same information, it is presented in a more informal manner. Course expectations and objectives are "discussed" with the reader. It reflects a different approach to presenting similar material.

Exhibit 4-2

Syllabus Example
Modified Traditional Model

(This approach uses a more informal style)

BIOLOGY

Winter 2006   Portland Adult Education

Instructor: Jamie MacDonald
Class meets Tuesdays and Thursdays 6-9 p.m. at Deering High School
Textbook: *Biology* by Maxine Lauren

This class is a GED/high school diploma course designed to survey biology. We will cover all basic biological ideas such as: cell structure and theory, life processes, human anatomy and physiology, botany, genetics, evolution, and ecology. There will be labs as a part of this course.

Because so much material is covered in a concentrated way, it is important that you make a commitment to attend class. More than two absences in a term will result in your not receiving credit for the course. If a special situation develops that will result in your missing a class, please discuss it with me.

In order to help you keep up with the material, there will be a quiz every week. This will help you to know where you stand and break the material up into smaller units. There will also be a mid-term and a final exam. On all quizzes and tests, it is the general concepts that are most important. Details can supplement your general understanding, but I will be asking you about the "big picture" rather than isolated facts. Questions will be short essays. This should guide your studying. Make-up quizzes will not be given. Each student can drop his or her lowest score from the final average. A missed quiz can be used as this dropped score. If you fail a quiz, you can rewrite it and submit it for a possible grade of 70. It is possible for everyone to pass this course if you attend regularly, and make up quizzes as needed.

Please feel free to ask any questions during class. Discussion helps us all understand and apply the information. If a question is too far off topic (this hardly ever happens), we'll talk about it after class is over. In order to provide time for individual help and questions, the lecture/discussion/lab part of the class will end at 8:30, but I will be available for help until 9:00.

As a part of this class, every student will choose a topic, research it, and present the information to the class. This will happen at the end of the semester. I will be giving you more information about this in a few weeks. We will also be doing article reports on topics related to current research in biology. I will give you more information about this as well.

Attached is a list of classes, topics to be covered, and chapters in the textbook that are on this particular topic. Reading the chapters before class will greatly improve your ability to understand the material. All material on quizzes and exams will be covered in class.

Biology is all about our world and how it is relevant to our lives. Most people find it interesting and relevant to their lives. *If there is anything I can do to help you enjoy and benefit from the class, please let me know.*

Course Schedule
(Subject to change)

Date	Topic	Reading
1/3/06	Introduction, Life Processes, Taxonomy	1,2
1/5/06	Cell, Theory, Cell Structure	
1/10/06	Cell Structure (cont.) chemistry	4
1/12/06	Chemistry (cont.)	4
1/17/06	Holiday	
1/19/06	Nutrition	5
1/24/06	Human Nutrition	11
1/26/06	Transport	6
1/31/06	Human Transport	12
2/2/06	Respiration	7
2/7/06	Human Respiration and Review	13
2/9/06	Mid-term Exam	
2/14/06	Vacation	
2/16/06	Vacation	
2/21/06	Excretion and Human Excretion	8,14
2/23/06	Regulation	9
2/28/06	Human Regulation	15
3/2/06	Locomotion and Human Locomotion	10,16
3/7/06	Asexual Reproduction—Mitosis	17
3/9/06	Sexual Reproduction—Meiosis	18,19
3/14/06	Genetics	20
3/16/06	Genetics (cont.)	20

3/21/06	Molecular Genetics	21
3/23/06	Evolution	23
3/28/06	Ecology	24
3/30/06	Final Exam	
4/4/06	Oral Reports	
4/6/06	Make-up class	

There are other approaches you can use when creating your syllabus. A general rule of thumb is a more informal course requires a less formal syllabus. If you are teaching a course in areas like art, cooking, or dance, you can modify your approach to meet your students' needs. Exhibit 4-3 shows how you can present course material in a more relaxed manner.

Syllabus Example
Informal Model

(Can be used for recreational/enrichment courses)

Easy Home Repair

Instructor: Libby Provencher
Course Hours: Saturday 9-11:00 a.m. (May 6-June 10, 2006)

Class #1 Tool Overview
Use hand and power tools to prep materials for future classes, wire, plywood, sheetrock, 2x4, and copper pipe.
Tools used, chalk line, square. saws, utility knife, wire cutters, hacksaw, pipe cutter.

Class #2 Fasteners
Identify and apply types of nuts and bolts, nails, screws, and anchors to

wood, metal, and concrete.
Drilling, riveting, clamping, countersinking, caulking, gluing, epoxy, plastic body filler, extractions, wooden plug.
Wood identification used for building a house.

Class #3 Electrical
Identify materials in home wiring.
Repair lamp and hook up outlet box.
Set tile on board for grouting in the next class. Cut tile and glass.

Class #4 Plumbing
Identify home plumbing materials,
Repair toilet, solder copper fitting, glue PVC.
Grout tile.

Class #5 Roofing and Siding
Identify materials used for the home.
Apply and replace asphalt and cedar shingles.
Aggregate identification.

Class #6 Masonry, Small Engine and Handy Hints
Mix mortar, butter brick, small engine maintenance.

Class #7 Meet at Home Depot Store

Clearly, syllabus Exhibit 4-3 meets the needs of a different type of class. The students taking a class in home repair certainly do not need the level of detail required in the other exhibits. In addition, administrative issues like attendance and grading may not be as critical for a class of this type versus the first two examples. Now let us examine another type of syllabus that combines the tone and style of the prior examples.

Exhibit 4-4 is unique in that it asks the student to fill in certain sections of the syllabus. This reflects an interesting approach in relation to the subject being taught. While it spells out key areas that are reflected in traditional syllabi, it also uses the more casual dialogue approach of Exhibit 4-2. This style syllabus is used often in adult education districts.

Exhibit 4-4

Syllabus Example
Informal-Academic Model

MATH CONCEPTS

Dates: _____

Number of School Days: _____

Day and Time: Monday and Wednesday, 9:00-11:30 a.m.

Teacher: Hi, my name is Jean Stovall and I've had the pleasure of teaching math to adults at Claremont Adult Education for a long time. Paula Mendell, my math colleague and I, have developed this course to help you pass the math GED or give you the necessary skills to prepare for applied algebra and then to be successful in college math.

Goals: My goals are to have you enjoy math through discovery and communicating with your peers, to rid you of any prior math anxieties, to have you experience some **fun**, and of course, to learn some math skills along the way.

Supplies You Will Need

1. Looseleaf notebook for your working portfolio.

2. A Sharp 509RHB Calculator. We sell them in the office for $ _____.

3. A pencil or many pencils!

What You Will Need To Do

1. **Homework** will be assigned every class from the text.

2. **Journal prompts** will be assigned after each class. Please respond to the questions assigned. Two journal entries for the week will be passed in on Mondays. I will respond to them and pass them back.

3. **Lab activities** will be done with a partner or in a small group. Once the activity is done, it is your responsibility to pass in the completed lab at the next class.

4. **Organization** is a must. You will need to organize your notebook into 5 sections.

      1) Homework Assignments

      2) Class Sheets/Notes

      3) Lab/Quizzes

      4) Journals

      5) Other: course outlines, learning style, etc.

5. Find a **math buddy**.

My math buddy is: _____
His or her phone number is: _____

The school phone number is: _____

6. **Attendance**. If you must miss a class, please call and leave a message for me. High School Diploma students may miss only _____ classes.

Enjoy the class!

We have presented you with several types of syllabi. As a new teacher, we recommend you begin with an existing syllabus if possible. At a minimum, you can use it as a guide to get you started in creating a syllabus that will meet your needs.

Your syllabus can serve a useful purpose in helping your students understand the expectations you have for the course. It can also serve as an instructional roadmap for both you and your students as the class progresses. Don't be afraid to get your students' input on its content. Is it clear? Does it meet their expectations? As you gain more teaching experience, you will continue to revise your syllabus to meet your needs and the needs of your students.

Chapter 5:
Choosing Books, Materials, and Assignments

In Chapter 4 we discussed how you plan a course and create a syllabus. In order to complete your planning, you will need to consider books, materials, and appropriate assignments to use. Here are some basic questions you need to consider when developing material for your class.

- Am I excited about the textbook?
- Should I use different books instead of one common text?
- Have I prepared my class in small segments so modifications can be made as the class progresses?
- Is there imagination exercised in developing lesson materials?
- Do I provide special lesson material to meet individual learning differences and styles?
- Am I versatile in the use of teaching devices and approaches?
- Do I prepare a plan for each class?

There are several strategies you can use to acquire books and materials for your course. Let's examine some of them.

Start with prior texts teachers used to teach the course. Many inexperienced teachers have started with existing texts. It is probably safe to say that most of us have used this as our starting point when we first taught. It can be challenging to create a new format for an existing class, especially if you have never taught before. Keep it simple, start with what others have used, and build from there. As you gain in experience and you get a better sense of students' abilities, you can make changes later on. The only exception is if the adult education director asks you not to use existing books. This can sometimes happen if the class has not worked in the past and the director wants a fresh start. There are several sources you can go to find new texts.

Talk to other teachers. This may seem fairly obvious but it is sometimes overlooked. If possible, talk to the teacher who taught the course prior to you. She or he can give you insights about the course, the text involved, and may provide you with other materials and assignments that can assist you.

Furthermore, try to contact teachers outside the district in which you will be teaching. They can give you even more insights, texts they use (different districts often use different texts), and additional resources.

Take time to explore the textbook room at your adult education office. Even if you use the existing text, we recommend you take some time to visit the textbook room at your local adult education office. Sometimes there are nooks and crannies where old books are stored. The textbook room can be a "goldmine" of potential material for your class. It often contains prior texts or handbooks used for your course. You may decide you like a book or two, ask to take them home and examine them carefully. These texts may provide you with great ideas for future assignments.

Use the Internet to look for new books and materials. The Web is a great resource for examining material. However, when you type in "adult education" you will be overwhelmed. If you are looking for new books, we suggest you start with a Web site like "The AcqWeb Directory." Web sites of this type will provide you with a full listing of adult education publishers and vendors. Sometimes, a publisher will even send you a sample copy. Call their toll free number and talk to them. One note, when we use the word "textbook" we are not just talking about the traditional textbook we are all familiar with. It can also mean a "workbook" or guidebook (which are common in adult education circles). Whatever text you end up using, it is critical that the book excites you! If you find excitement and value in the text, chances are good your students will respond to the book.

Another Web site that is popular with adult education teachers is ERIC (Education Resources Information Center). ERIC actually has multiple sites to explore. We have used ERIC to look for new reading material and to search for potential assignments and exercises for our students. You will find, however, that ERIC can be overwhelming in terms of the shear amount of resources to explore, so be prepared to spend some time looking for materials.

A third way to use the Web is to explore your subject with a direct search. Again, you may be inundated with information so think about key words that can focus your search directly to locations that can assist you.

Don't forget newspapers, magazines, and journals. Many teachers like to use newspapers and magazines. These resources can provide topical material for your students. Teachers in such diverse subjects as math, English, accounting, cooking, and many other subjects have told us they get a lot of material for their class exercises and assignments from newspapers and magazines. For example, math teachers often come across charts and graphs, English teachers find articles that provide useful scenarios to write about, and teachers in community enrichment courses (cooking, gardening, etc.) find "how to" articles and checklists that provide sources for new ideas and assignments in the courses they teach. Also, don't be afraid to use material gathered from your home. Any "real life" material you can utilize will provide students with more meaning in their learning experience.

Don't forget materials from your workplace (samples, examples, etc.). Most of us who teach for adult education have full-time jobs. We often teach subjects that are either closely related (or have great relevance) to our jobs. For example, if you find yourself teaching a class in business English, think about the different scenarios you have had to write about (i.e., responding to customer complaints, writing a letter to a vendor, various e-mails you've sent, etc.) "Real-life" examples provide so much more value and realism to your students than simply taking examples from a textbook. Don't be afraid to use the work of others from your workplace either. You can change names and situations to better complement your teaching goals. Just make sure you ask permission before you begin to use material that belongs to others.
If you are teaching a community enrichment course, we believe you will not have trouble finding appropriate assignments and projects for your students. In many cases, you will be teaching a class that is an avocation or hobby to you. Chances are you have already collected variety of material from a number of sources and have them at home. Bring the material to class to assist you.

Now let's take a look at various sample assignments that teachers have created for their classes. Our goal is to provide you with an overall sense of different approaches you can use to create assignments and lessons. As a new teacher, we suggest you start with your basic text (if applicable) and then expand toward more personalized assignments.

In the first three exhibits, we have taken assignments from three different computer classes. Note the different approaches you can use (projects, journal writing, and interactive student work) with your students.

Exhibit 5-1

Introduction to Personal Computers
Computer Project Ideas

As the course progresses, you will be asked to produce the following projects.
- Greeting cards
- Budgets
- Address book
- Financials for mortgage/car payments (monthly interest, new principal amounts)
- Balance checkbook
- Keep track of medical information
- Resumes/cover letters
- Keep track of birthdays, holidays, special events
- Recipes
- Catalog of collections (baseball cards, stamps, coins)
- To-do lists
- Brochures
- Car service maintenance records

Exhibit 5-1 is designed to give you examples of different projects students can create in their beginning computer class. Note the variety of projects with which students are presented. Students love to have options when it comes to projects. (For another project example, see Exhibit 5-6)

Exhibit 5-2 provides you with an assignment for another computer class but uses an entirely different approach. In this example, the teacher uses a common technique in adult education that calls for student writing/journalling. More and more adult education classes, from computers to math to communication skills are using journaling as an effective way to help students learn.

Remember, it is always better to give your student different ways to both learn and retain content.

Exhibit 5-2

Computers for Beginners
Journal Entry #2

Part A: Explain the steps needed to save a new document on the 3 ½ inch floppy for the first time. Then explain how you would open it up again if you wanted to work on it some other day.

Part B: Write a short definition of what functions the following computer keys enable you to do.

- Back Space

- Delete

- Enter

- Home

- End

- Ctrl Home

- Ctrl end

- Arrow Keys

Exhibit 5-3 gives you yet another type approach for a computer class. In this assignment, the teacher is requiring students to interact with each other in order to complete the assignment. We are giving you different scenarios for one class to show how assignments can differ, even for just one class.

It has been our experience that students gain tremendous meaning in their learning when they are actively engaged with fellow learners. Regardless of the class you are teaching, try to mix up your approaches.

Exhibit 5-3

**Computer Spreadsheets
Graphing Assignment**

Survey Question:

_____

_____

Category %	Category %	Category %	Category %

1. Ask members of the class your survey question. Keep track of their responses in the above table. Figure out the percentage that selected each category.

2. Enter the data into an Excel or Works spreadsheet table and then create two different graphs that show the information. Paste the charts into a word processing document and then analyze the data.

Another approach you can use is to get students directly involved by working in teams. Here is a different type of assignment for an office communication course. Note that in this exhibit, students are required to gather in small teams and use different methods to solve a problem. In addition, students are encouraged to use teaming skills to accomplish their tasks. When you mix up approaches, using small working groups can be an effective way to meet the diverse learning styles of your students.

Office Communication

(Teamwork Exercise)

No Frills Wear, Ltd.

Company Structure

Design Department
Creates new clothing lines. Uses input from the Marketing Department. Redesigns older clothes to keep them updated, especially those that sell. Recommends discontinuation of clothing lines that do not sell.

Business Department
Maintains financial records for all departments. Manages Accounts Receivable Department (collects money owed from customers/clients) and Accounts Payable (money paid out to vendors). Informs and advises about No Frills Wear, Ltd. expenditures and investments.

Marketing and Sales Department
Researches market trends and generating customer feedback. Responsible

for promoting company name and image, advertises products, sells products (company Web site, catalogue, other publications, TV, etc.), and customer service.

Production Department

Contracts with outside manufacturers to produce various clothing lines. Maintains warehouse for product inventory, ships clothing to customers.

The Challenge

The class will divide into small groups (4 students), which will be assigned one of the departments.

Using "brainstorming" and/or "mind mapping" techniques, each group must produce ideas for improving business in some way that will improve efficiency, reduce costs, and increase sales. Flip charts will be provided to each group to prepare their presentation to the entire class after one hour of small group work.

You can create different team-based assignments. In the following exhibit representing an Accounting I class, students are broken into groups to complete assigned tasks to gain a better understanding of basic accounting concepts. Note the complex interaction between content and how the groups are expected to use the material to develop additional ideas.

Exhibit 5-5

Accounting I
Class Simulation

1. This activity was created to show you how companies interact. Please make sure you have read Chapter 6 in your text so that you are familiar with:

> Chart of accounts
> Recording transactions in a five column journal
> Opening general ledger accounts and posting transactions
> Preparing a balance sheet

2. You will be divided into five groups; there are five companies in the activity.

3. Each group will be assigned a company. The companies are as follows:

> We Clean 4U - Main company
>
> Customers: Lobsta N'More
> Top Notch Rentals
>
> Vendors: Paperclip Office Supplies
> Quality Cleaning Products

4. Each group will also receive:
> Two journal copies
> Approximately eight copies of the general ledger
> One copy of the balance sheet

5. Each group will need to work together to complete the journal, open the general ledger accounts, post the journal to the general ledger, and prepare a balance sheet.

6. When completed, you will compare the five balance sheet reports and confirm that the customer and vendor balances crosscheck between companies.

7. Develop a class discussion on how these companies are related to each other. (e.g., What are the relationships between the transactions among the various companies?)

Besides using individual and team-based assignments, you can also use assignments that are project-based. Project work can be an extremely effective learning tool for your students. Note how Exhibit 5-6 is presented to students. Not only are the steps detailed and structured on how to proceed, the assessment is also included (see Chapter 14 for more details about assessment). Furthermore, students are asked to research a problem of interest to them, thereby adding relevance to their efforts.

Exhibit 5-6

Steps for Algebra Project

1. Statement of the problem you are researching

What have I observed that tells me that a problem exists?

Rewrite, in your own words, your explanation of what the problem is that you are attempting to solve. Example: You have noticed there are many Internet providers and it is confusing for the customer.

2. Question
What am I going to investigate?

It should be in question form. Example: Of three Internet companies picked, which plan would provide the consumer with the best deal?

3. Plan and method for collecting data

How am I going to gather information to answer this question?

Criteria for choosing data collection

      a. Will the information collected help answer your question?
      b. How much data will it give you and how much time will you need to analyze it?

4. Plan for analyzing data

What am I going to do with the data after I have gathered it?

For this project, some sort of graph is required, either scatter plots, curves, linear graphs, etc.

5. Findings

What did I find out? What is the answer to my question?

Explain how this problem fits in with other mathematical ideas you have studied. In particular, what concepts that you have learned since beginning applied Algebra have you incorporated into this problem? What does this problem leave you wondering about? What observations can you make about your results? What questions does the solution raise? In what ways could your strategy be used in a different situation?

6. Conclusion

What conclusions can you draw from your graphs and data collection? What does this mean for future implication?

7. Assessment

What do you believe you deserve for a grade on this report? I will provide you with a rubric that you will use to assess your presentation, written findings, and visuals. I will use the same rubric to also grade your project and presentation, the average of your assessment and mine will be your project grade. Remember, this project is worth 20% of your final grade.

8. Sample project suggestions:

Comparing telephone offers
Comparing Internet providers
How much electricity do you use?
Is the greenhouse effect growing?
Capital Gains: Using the Internet to investigate presidential campaign
    finances.
Interpreting opinion polls
Analyzing Baseball Hall of Fame statistics
Analyzing world population trends
Comparing leasing a car to buying a car
Choosing cell phone services and plans
Different investment options
Problems and causes of the growing teacher shortage in Maine

This exhibit is an outstanding example of how project work can be used to enhance student learning. Your ability to create and utilize effective assignments will go a long way in making the learning experience for your students a meaningful one. We suggest you provide students with a variety of lesson types and approaches. As you gain confidence and teaching experience, your arsenal of materials will increase. In our final exhibit, the teacher uses a creative method to teach measuring skills for students entering the metal trades. The assignment (building an envelope) has the added advantage of being flexible because it can be done individually or in groups of 2-3 students. Keep in mind that the students do not know what they are making. It adds a sense of excitement and curiosity to the exercise.

Exhibit 5-7

Metal Trades Lesson Plan

Competencies

Basic measurement
Basic math
Following directions
Precision

Materials Needed

1 pencil
1 yard stick and ruler
1 piece flip chart paper, measuring 26 $7/8$" X 32 $11/16$"
rubber cement or glue stick
scissors

Directions

1. Find the center of the page.

2. Make a light mark.

3. Position the paper horizontally in front of you on a flat surface.

4. Lightly draw a horizontal rectangle centered around the center mark and measuring 5 $1/2$" x 8 $1/2$".

5. Drawing with a dark line, extend the vertical lines at the bottom right and left corners of the rectangle to an additional 3".

6. From your center reference, measure down 7", parallel with the vertical lines, and make a light mark.

7. Draw two dark lines from the 7" mark to each end of the 3" lines.

8. Turn your paper around, so that it is horizontal, but what you just drew is on top.

9. Repeat steps 5-7.

10 Turn your paper to a vertical position.

11. Extend each vertical line at the bottom corners of the rectangle 1" using a dark line.

12. From the center reference, measure down 8" and make a light mark.

13. Connect the ends of the 1" lines to the 8" mark with a dark line.

14. Turn the paper around, so that what you just drew is on the top and the paper is vertical.

15. Repeat steps 11-13.

16. Use the scissors to cut out the drawing along the dark lines.

17. Fold toward the center along each of the four sides of the original rectangle.

18. Unfold the flaps. Place the paper in a horizontal position.

19. Fold the bottom flap up.

20. Beginning at the fold, apply 1/4" strip of glue to the lower edges of the right and left flaps, out 1" then up the angled side to the point.

21. Fold right and left flaps onto outside of bottom flap and gently press so glue will adhere.

22. Final product must fit within a 3/8" tolerance.

The purpose of this chapter was to give you a sense of the various resources available to you to create appropriate assignments and locate the necessary books and materials for you to use in your class. As a new teacher, we expect you will first depend on quite a bit of material used in prior classes. This is an entirely acceptable strategy to use; in fact, we encourage it. We wanted to supplement this strategy with some ideas and approaches that will provide meaningful assignments for your students. Use your imagination! The nice thing about teaching is that if a particular lesson does not work for a class, you can put it aside and move on. However, be cautious about what you throw away after a negative experience. We have seen a lesson or assignment not work for one class and operate nicely with another. Each class will be unique and have a different group of people with their own personalities and learning styles. Unless the assignment is an unmitigated disaster, we suggest you try it again. Remember to "check in" with students after assignments are finished. They are often your best critics and will help you make adjustments for future assignments and projects.

Chapter 6:
The First Class

You're about to enter your first classroom as an adult educator. Are you feeling nervous? Elated? Apprehensive? Excited? Or just plain scared? Even the most experienced adult educator had to face their first class at some point. Walking into your first classroom can produce a whole series of emotions. Teachers have reflected on their first class experience as a combination of riding a roller coaster, a horse, or an airplane for the first time. In other words, a mix of emotions, including excitement coupled with apprehension, and even fear. However, all teachers have endured this experience. You are not alone.

The first class sets the tone for the entire semester, and it is your opportunity to establish a supportive, positive learning experience and environment for students. This is critical because adult education, by nature, is one of the most democratic experiences you will encounter. Adult education students, for example, often come to school voluntarily, know what they are looking for, can be impatient, and need a comfortable learning environment. Adult students vote with their feet. If they find value in their initial experience, they will probably return. If they don't, they won't. This is why the first class can be a challenging experience for even the seasoned adult educator.

Good planning will help by alleviating, or at least minimizing, some of your fears and concerns. The more planning you put into the initial class, the more organized (and better) you will feel as you walk through the door. Also, remember that however anxious you are, your students are equally if not more frightened. Here are some ideas to consider.

First, try to visit the classroom a day or two prior to your start date. Is it a traditional room with individual tabletop desks? Or, does it have longer tables with chairs. Can you adjust the tables or chairs to form a square or circle? Will you be teaching in a larger common-area room that is partitioned with cubicle type walls? Having a better sense of your teaching environment will help you plan and alleviate some of your own fears about the unknown. An important note: If you decide to alter the physical nature of the room, please remember to return the room to its former state after class is over. If you do not, you may find an unpleasant note waiting for you from the school administrator or teacher when you return to teach again. No one likes to see their work area altered.

Second, check to see if your student roster (attendance sheet) is prepared a day or so prior to your start date. Call ahead to the adult education office to see if you can pick it up when you visit the classroom. The combination of the number of students enrolled, coupled with the type of room you will teach, can be critical to how you design the first session. How you start off a larger group (ten or more students) might vary from your approach with a smaller one (six students or less). Be prepared for late "add-ons" to the student roster. Some adult education programs will enroll students right up to the start of class.

On class day, arrive 15-20 minutes early. This will allow time to set your materials out for easy access and greet students as they arrive. Remember to smile; nothing helps put students at ease more than a smile. In many ways, the principle is identical to interviewing for a job. Your body language and demeanor will be better served with a smile on your face. This has an immediate positive impact on the learning environment you are trying to develop.

If possible, try to seat yourself among the students (this is where a circle or squared seating arrangement is helpful). If you are teaching where only traditional classroom seating is offered (e.g., high school rooms and some computer labs are often set up this way), try your best not to start off with students being seated in the traditional manner. If possible, try moving seats into an initial discussion circle. Computer courses are notorious, because the terminals act as defensive shields for students to hide behind. Some computer classes have large worktables located in the same room. You may want to start there.

Introduce yourself, and write your name and the course title on the board. Don't worry about attendance right away; there will be plenty of time for that later. Some students may come a little late if they don't know where the classroom is. As they arrive, give them a friendly greeting. They will often feel awkward and uneasy.

If you feel nervous, let the students know. Many teachers have expressed their anxious feelings to the class, using it as an opportunity to talk about everyone learning together. This can reduce student apprehensions and fears by reminding them they are not alone in their feelings. Even experienced teachers can use this as an opportunity to relax.

Have plenty of blank paper or old manila folders and markers for students (and yourself) to make nameplates. These can be made with students writing their names in large print and folding the paper (or folders). Some teachers like to use stick-on nametags instead of nameplates. Use your best judgment. Addressing each other by first name is another small step that helps to develop a "learning community." Spend a few minutes briefly describing the course. You can hand out the syllabus later after introductions have been made using an *icebreaker* exercise.

There are some common elements to consider in the first class. These are:
- Establishing a safe learning environment
- Introducing yourself, students, and class content
- Getting a sense of how your students learn and their current abilities

One approach you can use is introducing an effective *icebreaker* exercise. An icebreaker is an interactive exercise that can help you and your students get introduced, establish a safe learning environment, begin to get a sense of how your students learn, and how they feel about the class. Exhibits 6-1 and 6-2 provide examples of icebreaker exercises.

In the following exercise, students "interview" each other and then introduce their partner to the larger class. The exercise can be tailored to reflect the specific course you teach. (Exhibit 6-2)

Exhibit 6-1

General Icebreaker Exercise
"Introductions"

1. What is the name of the person to whom you are talking?

2. Have them tell you a little about themselves. Where were they born? How many children do they have? What school did they last attend?

3. Do they have a hobby? If so, what?

4. What is their favorite ice cream? If they don't like ice cream, what is their favorite food?

5. How would they describe their learning style? How do they learn best? Writing/taking notes? Reading? Doing? Listening? Drawing charts?

6. If they could take a trip anyplace in the world, where would they like to go?

7. Do they have any concerns or fears about the class? Is there anything the class can do to help them overcome it?

8. What do they hope to get out of the class? What are their learning goals?

Enjoy the class everyone!

The purpose of the icebreaker is to help students begin to become comfortable with each other and the course. This exercise works best when you have over eight students but you can modify the exercise to meet your individual needs. It also works best if you participate in the exercise; so an odd number of students will work to your advantage.

Having students introduce each other is a relatively non-threatening way to get them to begin to talk to each other individually and collectively. It also provides you with an initial indication on how your students may learn and what they hope to get out of the class. As students introduce each other using the icebreaker exercise, it is important to ask follow-up questions as the questions are discussed. While some questions may appear frivolous, they are not. It is important to give the students a chance to relax and have fun. You may want to write down the learning goals and/or styles as they are presented. This will help you collect your thoughts for discussions regarding the syllabus later on. The students will also draw connections between their expectations and the course content.

The second icebreaker example is designed for a specific class (Business English) and can be individually completed by the student or with the same interview format as the first icebreaker exercise. Used as an individual exercise, upon completing the icebreaker questionnaire, students introduce themselves to the class using the exercise as a prompt to share a little about themselves and what they hope to accomplish in the course.

Exhibit 6-2

Icebreaker Exercise
Business English

Your name: _____

Please answer the following questions:

1. Do you have any experience writing business correspondence? If so, what type?

2. If you left this class learning only three things about Business English, those three things would be?

3. Do you have any fears concerning this class? If so, what are they? How can we help you overcome them?

4. How do you learn best? By doing? Taking notes? Listening?

5. What is your favorite type of food?

Enjoy the class!

A well-conducted icebreaker can establish a positive, supportive learning environment for the students and begin the process of reducing apprehension by addressing their fears and providing you with some critical information about each students' expectations and learning style. We have seen other icebreaker exercises that involve such fun activities as scavenger hunts or having students work as partners on specific exercises. There are many different types of things you can do. You can find examples of specific icebreakers in such books as *The Winning Trainer* (Eitington, 1996).

After the icebreaker exercise, it may be the appropriate time to introduce your syllabus and any administrative information that may be critical to the students. (e.g., attendance policy, breaks, parking, rules on smoking, access to the building at night). Effectively communicating your expectations is critical for students. They have come to class because they expect something from you. Remember to focus on the course objectives and goals. It may be appropriate to refer back to some of the comments made during the icebreaker exercise so that you can draw connections between student expectations and what the course expects to deliver.

Next, you may want to have the students help establish ground rules on how the class will be conducted. This exercise can help create a positive, safe learning environment. When students feel like they have a voice in the establishment of guidelines, they believe the course has been designed, in part by them, for them. With a large group, you may want to break students into smaller teams to help facilitate this type of activity. You can even include a "strict" brainstorming activity rule that gives all students a chance to participate. You can begin this exercise by asking lead questions such as "What rules do we want to set for ourselves to guide the course?" or "What tone do we want to set for the class. How can we create this tone?" or even "What are your specific learning objectives for this course?" The teacher can then write down the student responses on the board or flip charts.

Examples of ground rules may include but are not limited to:
- Trust and mutual respect
- Don't interrupt
- Focus on the issue, not the person
- Actively participate
- Listen attentively
- Keep confidences
- Encourage questions and sharing
- Be honest
- Respect boundaries and each other's space
- Value diversity

Remember that each class is different and ground rules will be developed based on the type of course you teach and the students' own personal experiences. It is important that you facilitate this discussion and help guide it, but allow students the freedom to express themselves.

Creating a *first class agenda* is a great way to keep organized and focused. The agenda can be modified to meet the needs of any scenario. Exhibit 6-3 is a "First Class Agenda" you can use as an initial guide.

Exhibit 6-3

First Class Agenda

1. Welcome
2. Introduce yourself
3. Announcements
4. Brief description of course
5. Icebreaker Exercise
    Student introductions
    Student concerns, fears
    Learning styles, objectives

6. Introduce syllabus, goals, expectations

Break

7. Group activity—establishing a positive learning environment

8. Summary of material and questions from students

Keep in mind that the number of students you have will influence how long your first class agenda will take. In general, more students equate to more comments and questions. After you have covered the material in the agenda, you may have time to begin your first lesson plan.

More than anything else, enjoy yourself in the first class. Have fun with it! It is an exciting, exhilarating experience for every teacher (new and otherwise), and it sets the tone for a productive, pleasant learning experience for you and students. A rewarding first class provides students with the emotional support to continue on. In addition, by honoring the democratic nature of the adult education experience, students are inclined to return for another day of learning.

Chapter 7:
Establishing a Safe Environment for Learning

In the previous chapter, we briefly discussed the importance of establishing a safe learning environment for your students in the first class. As a teacher, this is one of the critical elements you need to consider constantly as your class progresses.

There is a simple relationship between the comfort students feel versus their ability to learn. Here are some questions you should consider.

- Do my students feel welcome?
- Is the classroom physically comfortable?
- Do I know the names of my students?
- Am I alert in keeping students engaged? Do I utilize various types of individuals, small and large group activities?
- Do I create an atmosphere in which, "we will learn something of value?"
- Is there a cooperative learning atmosphere?

Your ability to create a learning environment that is safe, engaging, cooperative, and productive will go a long way in making your students feel they are getting real value from your class. We have spoken to a number of our students about what they look for in a safe learning environment and they have mentioned many factors. Here are some "ground rules and needs" they have mentioned.

- Encourage everyone to participate.
- Make sure people don't interrupt when others are speaking.
- Make sure people focus on the issue during classroom discussion and not the person talking.
- Listen to your students.
- Confidentiality is essential for people to feel safe in expressing themselves
- Learn your students' names.
- Encourage questioning and sharing.

- Show humility.
- Balance intervening versus allowing student dialogue.
- Insist on an air of honesty in the classroom.
- Bring a sense of humor to class.
- Emphasize that students need to get to know each other.
- Encourage trust and mutual respect between the teacher and learners.
- Value diversity so everyone can learn.
- Students must feel safe that "it's okay" to ask questions.
- The teacher (and students) need to mutually respect the boundries of fellow students.

We know we are presenting you with quite a list of things to ponder and consider, but don't fret. Even the most experienced teacher needs to remind her/himself constantly that maintaining a safe learning environment for students requires constant vigilance and dedication. Let's take a look at these "ground rules" and examine them a little closer.

Encourage everyone to participate. Your ability to get as many people as possible to express themselves in your class will add meaningful texture to the learning experience for all students. Not everyone will want to talk, but set up formats that encourage dialogue. As students get more comfortable, try things like "round robin" dialogues in which you go around the room asking people for their opinion on a specific topic. This technique provides those who would not normally raise their hand to join the conversation. Respectfully accept the decision of those who may not want to comment.

Make sure people don't interrupt when others are speaking. This can cause real problems if allowed to go uncontrolled. Constant interruptions can disrupt the natural flow of peoples' ideas and thoughts. One way to control the situation passively is to use body language to help people wait before they talk. A simple movement of your finger to your mouth along with a smile can go a long way in reminding students to wait and let others finish. At other times, a direct approach is more effective. Politely ask people to speak only when other students are finished.

Make sure people focus on the issue during classroom discussions and, not the person talking. It is important that students remember that everyone has opinions and has the right to express them. Students need to keep personalities out of the dialogue when classroom discussions occur.

Listen to your students. This may sound simple, but we have experienced those times when we are caught up in presenting content and lose sight of what students may be saying to us. We sometimes call this the problem of "self-talk." Keep your ears open!

Confidentiality is essential for people to feel safe in expressing themselves. When students know they can share openly with others without being judged, the classroom becomes a better learning environment. Students begin to feel emotionally safe. When working with students "at risk," this is especially important. A particularly challenging and sensitive area is when students get into personal topics that indicate they are in dangerous situations (i.e., physical/emotional abuse, drug or alcohol abuse, etc.). Your local administrator will have specific protocols to follow if confronted with these issues.

Learn your students' names. This can be a real challenge for many teachers, especially if you are memory challenged like us or if your class has more than five students. We recommend that you use name tags/plates to help you. Nameplates can be particularly effective because you can collect them at the end of the first class and use them for the next few classes to help everyone get acquainted.

Encourage questioning and sharing. Students should feel safe to ask questions when necessary. As the old adage goes, "there are no dumb questions." Furthermore, students need to believe they have the right to share. Simple things like calling on students by name can go a long way in making them feel comfortable. Making sure students do not mock or belittle the comments of others will also create an environment of cooperation and the free exchange of ideas.

Show humility. What do we mean by this? Simply, as teachers, we will make mistakes, and we do not know everything. A common fear for teachers is that they are asked a question and have no answer. Relax, you will not know everything about your subject. It's okay to say, "I don't know but I will get you an answer." Confidence sprinkled with a pinch of humility makes a powerful recipe toward a comfortable learning environment. Conversely, perceived arrogance, inflexibility, or intimidation on the part of the teacher is a recipe for disaster.

Balance intervening versus allowing student dialogue. There may be times when the dialogue in your class drifts away from the topic at hand. You must devise a way to work your way politely into the conversation and get people back on track.

Insist on an air of honesty in the classroom. Students will respond when they know that the conversations generated in your classroom are open and honest. Honesty corresponds directly to your ability to gain the respect of your students. Being honest and direct with students does not, however, correlate to being brutal, hostile, or overly critical in feedback. Always be respectful to your students.

Bring a sense of humor to class. Humor is one of your main allies in working with adults. Your students have lived, and they bring a wealth of experience to the classroom. Adult learners did not come to your class to moan and be unhappy. People appreciate a more relaxed learning atmosphere and humor can help you.

Emphasize that students need to get to know each other first. Before students can feel safe, they need to get a sense of who is in their class. As they get to know each other, they relax and better learning can occur. The first class can help with this. Use an exercise or two within the first couple of classes to generate familiarity among students.

Encourage trust and mutual respect between the teacher and learners. This occurs through many of the practices listed above. However, we would add that students must feel as though the teacher will be fair to them in how class is conducted. When students feel they are treated fairly, their teachers gain in prestige and respect.

Value diversity—everyone can learn. We have had the privilege of teaching in classes with students from around the world. Students from other countries bring tremendous life experiences to their classrooms and their classmates. The breadth of these experiences adds value to the learning experience for everyone. We often use the strategy of deliberately grouping students from various backgrounds into small working groups to enhance the learning experience for everyone in the class.

Students must feel safe that "it's okay" to ask questions. In their earlier educational history, some students were punished for asking questions. This should never happen in adult education. Be sure to let everyone know their questions are welcome. We strongly recommend you make it clear in your syllabus and on the first day of class that questions are encouraged.

The teacher (and students) need to respect the boundaries of fellow students. This is important factor to keep in mind. Students may take some time in opening up. They need to feel safe in their own space until they feel ready to join larger group discussions. Sometimes, gently prodding can help but don't be overpowering in your approach. In addition, different students have different personal boundaries. Everyone needs to feel safe, otherwise students will stop trusting each other and you.

It is impossible to always honor each of the items on this list all the time. Even the best teacher makes mistakes when it comes to establishing a safe learning environment. Our recommendation is that you carefully go over this list and make some preliminary decisions on how you might approach each of these factors based on your personality and style. Teachers have different styles. You discover your style in making the learning experience a meaningful and productive one for your students.

Chapter 8:
The Art and Science of Lectures

Many of us grew up on lectures. That is, the primary way we were taught in grade school, high school, and college was by our teachers lecturing or presenting information. Most likely one of the ways we came to judge "good" from "bad" teachers was how informative and interesting they made their lectures.

In adult education circles, lecturing does not always receive a warm reception. After all, adult education is supposed to be student-centered and participatory. The best adult educators are far less concerned with their "performance" in front of a class than they are with getting students to participate actively in their own learning. And numerous studies that have compared the effectiveness of lectures as compared with other teaching methods—especially discussion—yield discouraging results. As McKeachie (2002) reports, discussion methods are superior to lectures in student retention of information after the end of a course, transfer of knowledge to new situations, development of problem solving, and motivation for further learning.

So why bother? Why include a chapter in this book about the art and science of lecturing? The answers are numerous. Lectures are still a highly useful way for the teacher to present up-to-date information on the subject being taught (there is typically a gap of two years or more between the most current information and its availability in even a recently published book). They are excellent summary tools, tying together loose ends of issues being taught. Lectures can help students read more effectively by providing an orientation and conceptual framework. And a well-presented lecture can have rich motivational value if the student picks up from her/his teacher an excitement and passion for the subject matter at hand. On good days we have had students comment to us after a lecture. "Wow—I didn't realize this area was as interesting as it now appears" or "Thank you for bringing these complex ideas into greater clarity for me."

Planning Your Lecture

Here are some things to consider when you are planning a lecture.

- *Never plan to lecture the entire class period.* Even if your class only lasts 45 or 60 minutes, this is far too long to be talking to your students. Research indicates that human beings have an attention span of between 10 and 20 minutes (and with some people it's even shorter!). Make plans to change the activity approximately every 15 minutes to relieve monotony and maintain students' interest. For example, design into your lecture time for small group problem solving, have students write a "minute paper" through which they get a chance to express their understanding of the topic being taught, or introduce an entirely different way of presenting content (e.g., film clip, printed handout, music, etc.).

- *Outline lecture modules.* The inexperienced teacher might find it helpful to actually have a list of modules (learning units) with time parameters for a lecture-based class. It is not always necessary to share this outline with students, although we believe it is generally good practice to do so (this can be done in the form of a printed handout or by writing out the units of time on a black/white board or flip chart). An example of lecture modules from a class on the History of World War II might look like this:

Topic for Tonight's Class: June 6, 1944 (D-Day)

7:00 Welcome! Ask for comments about last week's reading assignment

7:15 Lecture - Issues in planning the invasion of France

7:30 "Minute Paper" - We'll actually make this a "Five Minute Paper" tonight. Write about what you feel was the single biggest problem General Eisenhower faced in planning the D-Day invasion. Ask for volunteers to read their paper.

7:45 Group Discussion of "Minute Papers"

8:00 Break

8:15   *15-minute video clip from beginning of "Saving Private Ryan"*

8:30   *Working in groups of three, discuss feelings about this dramatic representation of the invasion*

9:00   *Lecture on the Atlantic Wall and other defensive strategies by the Germans*

9:15   *Questions and advance-organizer for next class*

Having an outline that shows where learning modules will be placed within the context of the entire class will help you to manage the evening and—if you share it with students—will help them have a sense of how the class is going to be organized (while there might be an exception or two, most students like to know what's going to happen over the course of a two or two and one-half hour class). However, be prepared to be flexible. You might have to make adjustments.

Prepare notes but do not read from a "script." There is an irony of etymology here. While the word "lecture" derives from the Latin "lectus/legere" which means to read, the one thing you do not want to do is to read, literally, a script to your students. In fact, reading more than an occasional paragraph, poem, or some other brief narrative is just about the worst way to approach a lecture. Among other things, reading a script detracts from your ability to establish eye contact and forces your own voice downward. It is also extremely time-consuming to write out lectures word for word. "Talking notes" may be either general or well-detailed depending on your own comfort level with the material being taught. If you have taught a subject before (or work with it every day) and know a lot about it, a few key words might be sufficient. This is something you will have to experiment with and over time you will establish your own unique style of preparing your lecture notes. A sample of lecture notes is provided in Exhibit 8-1.

Teach to multiple senses. Lectures are primarily designed for the ears. Consequently, they can be a wonderful teaching-learning tool for those of us who are auditory learners. However, not all of us learn best by listening. An effective adult educator will pay attention to the multiple ways humans learn and will plan to design activities that involve other senses. Accompanying one's lecture with overhead transparencies of key ideas, or a colorful handout, or writing on a black/white board, will accent the presentation in such a way as to interest even those who are not auditory learners. If an appropriate situation arises providing some kind of "hands on" activity that will literally involve touch will directly invite tactile learners into the learning circle. We've said this in other places in this book: variety is an important spice and can make the difference between reaching all versus only some of your adult students.

Structure your lecture to help students remember the most important material. Research has shown that people retain the most at the beginning of a presentation. Retention declines toward the middle and rises again in anticipation of the end (Davis, 1993). Plan your lecture so that the main points come at a time when students are most attentive. This may include (1) an outline of modules as noted above to show the overall plan of the class, (2) an attention-getting introduction, (3) frequent summaries, including opportunities for the learners to synthesize for themselves what they are understanding, (4) concluding summary of major points to reinforce the key themes of the lesson.

Prepare mentally and emotionally. What the teacher does during the 30 minutes just prior to class may be among the most important preparations she or he can make. It is not advisable to walk "cold" into our classroom and immediately start to teach. Some individuals require a few minutes of reflection beforehand (in their car, or in an office) to center thoughts and focus energy and attention. Others prefer to take a brief walk in order to relax physically. Most teachers like to go into the classroom 10 or 15 minutes early and be sure the room is set up correctly and necessary equipment is ready. This also provides an opportunity to talk informally with students who have also arrived early. Relaxed and informal conversation before the start of class often transitions into a relaxed start of a lecture. If you are feeling comfortable, chances are your students will be, too.

Delivering Your Lecture

If you have planned your lecture well, the chances are excellent that it will go well. However, to increase that probability, here are a number of suggestions from our own teaching practice for maximizing the potential of lectures.

Involve students early. Ask an engaging question. Tell a story (have you ever considered how magical the four words, "Once upon a time," are?). Get students to stand up and form a circle. Give them a brief questionnaire to complete. Mention a recent news event. Make a brief demonstration. Show a picture. In other words, use the opening moments of your lecture to invite students into the learning. But be sure not to repeat even the best opening again and again. Any dramatic technique loses impact upon repetition. Here are several examples:

- (for a criminal justice/sociology lecture) "How many people would you guess are sent to prison every day in the United States?"
- (for a class in public speaking). "True or false: The greatest fear among Americans is speaking in front of a group of people. If you think this statement is true, why? If you think it is false, why?"
- (for a class on human memory). "Watch what happens when I pour water from this pitcher into the beaker which already has water in it."
- (for a unit in office communication). "I recently had to help resolve a conflict between two employees. Here's what happened (tells story of the conflict). Now before I tell you what I did, what would you do if faced with this situation?"
- (for a class in social gerontology). "Today our main topic is to explore social and psychological theories of aging. Let me begin by asking you a question: what is a theory?"
- (for a class on sports and society). "I've made an enlargement of a recent cartoon from *The New Yorker* that depicts a football. What do you think (show the cartoon) this means?"
- (for a class in economics). "I've brought in last Sunday's newspaper where there was a feature article about local dairy farmers pouring thousands of gallons of fresh milk into the ground (reads first paragraph and shows headline). Why do you think farmers did this?"

- (for a course in business English). "I've brought in a piece of junk mail I recently received. Let's see what errors we can locate in this document."

Orient and Connect. As we have already discussed, providing an outline (perhaps with specific time allocations) on the board, flip chart, or handout will help to orient students to what is about to happen. It provides a whole view of where you will be going as a community of learners. As part of this introduction, it is often advisable to make connections to material that has already been covered in this course of study. In other words, where have we journeyed thus far and how does tonight's material fit into the entire story of the course?

Use Examples. Examples irrigate thought. They also tend to be remembered more than facts and theories. Bring as many salient examples into your lecture as you can. As you gain experience in teaching you will increase the number of examples you have in your teacher's tool box. Remember, if you are teaching a subject that is closely related to your full-time work, you will probably have numerous examples to draw upon. However, to "protect the innocent," please remember to alter or delete altogether the real names of persons you may mention in your example.

Check in continually. It makes no sense to be lecturing if your students don't have a clue what you're talking about. Yet, some teachers—perhaps more interested in their own "performance" than students' learning—push on and do this very thing. A remedy for this compulsion is to put into your lecture notes reminders to check students' understanding—both by looking for nonverbal cues of bewilderment or of lack of attention and by asking them questions. Again, simple devices like the "Minute Paper" (see chapter 14) are a good way of checking in to see what, if anything, people are learning. Another strategy is to facilitate a quick round robin (literally going from student to student in order of their seating) and ask for one big idea each person has learned thus far in this class. Round robin reporting is more public than a one-minute paper and runs the risk of someone not being able to come up with a response and, hence, feeling embarrassment. But the pressure can be diffused by allowing people to "pass" if they do not feel ready to respond. The specific culture of your class and the quality of the relationships in the group will help to determine whether or not you might take this risk.

Vary the type of lectures you deliver. Lectures are not always the same, nor should they be. At times you may wish to treat a single question or problem in an *expository* presentation. This is the traditional type of lecture where you have a well-organized presentation with major and minor points about the subject at hand. It's okay to do this every once in awhile, but don't become overly dependent on expository-type lectures, because they risk transforming your students into passive spectators. At times you may wish to employ the use of *interactive* lectures that involve questions, answers, and dialogue and sometimes represent a kind of orderly brainstorming. There are also *problem-solving* lectures where you pose a question or paradox ("What would happen if…") that whet students' interest. And there are also *case study* lectures where you present a situation (it may be real or fictional) that serves to illustrate a general principle or overriding idea you are trying to teach.

Vary the presentation itself. Talking is important. Much teaching takes place through the use of words. But as we've noted in numerous places in this book, teaching has come a long way since the days when instructors talked (constantly) and students sat dutifully and listened. The more we can bring color, music, activity, dialogue, film, and other accents that are appropriate into the mix of our teaching, the richer and more vital the experience will be for everyone. It's true that most teachers feel comfortable working with one or two presentation styles (e.g., some folks are awesome doing PowerPoint while others are great storytellers). But if you are willing to move a little out of your early comfort zone—your "natural" teaching style—and take some risks in the way you lecture, you will end up having more fun and your students will both enjoy themselves and benefit from your varied practice.

Summarize periodically. Summaries are useful for a number of reasons. First, they reiterate important information and thus, through a practice effect, help to enhance retention. Second, they allow students who may be taking notes to catch their breath and, if they have fallen a little behind, catch up (it is extremely frustrating to feel rushed and have the sense that one is constantly behind). Third, a summary helps the learner check on possible misperceptions she or he may have had about the content. And finally, a summary also helps the teacher. If you can provide a cogent synopsis of the main points of a lecture, you can be reasonably confident that you understand the material and can communicate it (nice things to know as a teacher!).

Obtain feedback on your lectures and reflect on it. The good adult educator seeks feedback and wants to improve her/his teaching. Ask your students at various intervals what they like and do not like about your lectures. If you keep a personal diary, use a recent teaching experience as a focal point for an entry. If the adult education program in which you teach offers opportunities for peer observation (e.g., one teacher sitting in as a guest to observe another teacher), take advantage of it. And volunteer to be a peer observer for one of your colleagues—we can learn a great deal about teaching (both lecturing and many other aspects of this work) by paying close attention to another teacher's practices. Finally—and this is a big risk for some people—try video-taping your lecture. Take the tape home, review it, and look for ways in which you can improve. Videotapes will provide us with the most honest feedback we'll ever get! As you review your tape, you may want to evaluate yourself using a self-assessment checklist such as the one we offer in Exhibit 8-2.

Be Yourself. This is probably the best advice we can give. There is a tendency in a new teacher to try to emulate successful practices that we've observed in others—perhaps a favorite college professor or some other great teacher we have known. Teaching, because it is ultimately an extension of our personality and character, needs to come from one's authentic self. If you are a quiet person, believe that you can teach "quietly" but nonetheless as effectively as an extrovert can. If you naturally use a lot of hand gestures when you speak, accept that and don't attempt to change (and if gestures are not something that come easily and naturally to you, accept that as well and don't force yourself to add them to your teaching repertoire). Being yourself as you plan and deliver your lecture—and as you teach in all other ways—is the best gift you can give both yourself and your students.

Exhibit 8-1

Lecture Notes on the Topic: Is Baseball America's "National Pastime"?

(This is approximately a one-hour course module)

1. *(Opening - 5 minutes) Baseball has been called America's "National Pastime" since the Civil War. We'll get into the question of whether baseball still is America's pastime later in this class, but let's look briefly at the historical foundations for this assertion. Ask the class: "Why do you think the game of baseball won this moniker to begin with?" Record student responses on board.*

2. *(5 minutes) It isn't merely a matter of chronology. Football, basketball, golf, tennis, ice hockey, boxing all existed in the 19th century (briefly describe).*

3. *(5 minutes) Tell the story of Albert Spalding, The Mills Commission, and the making of baseball's creation myth*

4. *(30 minutes) G. Edward White has written an important book about key developments between 1900 and 1950 that more or less cemented the idea that baseball was America's National Pastime (pass around White's book, Creating the National Pastime). Here are some of the key points the author makes in his argument:*
   - *Steel and concrete ballparks (built between 1908 - 1923) gave a sense of permanency and helped to develop community identity and pride around their team (ask students if they can name some of these parks—list on board)*
   - *Increased prominence in society of newspapers generally and the sports page in particular*
   - *The development of a "world" series (beginning in 1903). Ask the class - who played in the first world series? What happened in 1904 for what should have been a second world series?*
   - *The development and spread of radio (1920's and 30's)*
   - *1933 - the first All Star Game*
   - *Ethnic inclusiveness (moving from mostly WASPs to Irish and Germans in the early part of the 20th Century and later to Italians and Jews)*
   - *Racial inclusiveness (Jackie Robinson and the Dodgers)*
   - *Creation of a National Baseball Hall of Fame and Museum*

5. *(15 minutes)* Read the following quote and ask students to respond to it in a "Minute" Paper (allow five minutes for writing):

Young people today are bombarded with sports, both at the level of participation and observation. Many sports are easier to play than baseball. As fewer young Americans play baseball because of competition from other sports, and fewer American families are financially able to attend games regularly, the time-honored customs of parents playing catch with their children or taking them to the park to watch their heroes may give way to other rituals. It may be that the 21st Century will be one in which commentators gravely announce that baseball was, rather than is, America's national pastime.

After writing, ask for volunteers to read their "Minute Paper" and/or talk about their response to the quote.

Exhibit 8-2

An Instrument for Evaluating a Lecture or Presentation

Note: This instrument may be used in a variety of ways: (1) Look over variables and try to keep them in mind while you plan and deliver your lecture (2) Have students use this instrument from time to time to evaluate your lecture (3) Videotape yourself (we recommend you do this at least once per year) and then, while reviewing the video, use this instrument.

Peer Evaluation of Lecture / Presentation

Facilitator's Name _____ Evaluator's Name _____

Please circle one response for each item: 4 = excellent, 3 = good, 2 = needs some attention, and   1 = needs significant attention
Note: If an item is "not applicable" (e.g., "used technology appropriately" when no technologies were used), please leave it blank.

Introduction

Introduced self to class   4 3 2 1

Established "ground rules" for participation   4 3 2 1

Provided an outline of the subject being presented   4 3 2 1

Other comments about the introduction _____

_____

Body of the Lecture / Presentation

The content was clearly presented   4 3 2 1

The overall logic (organization) was sound   4 3 2 1

Pace of speech	4 3 2 1
Volume of speech	4 3 2 1
Variety of speech (pitch, etc.) for emphasis	4 3 2 1
Hand gestures	4 3 2 1
Eye contact	4 3 2 1
Involved learners as part of the presentation	4 3 2 1
Moved purposefully (not "pacing" or stuck to lectern)	4 3 2 1
Showed genuine interest or enthusiasm in the topic	4 3 2 1
Appeared knowledgeable/comfortable with the content	4 3 2 1
Used technology appropriately	4 3 2 1
Time management	4 3 2 1
Was engaging and helped me to learn	4 3 2 1

Other comments about the body of the presentation_____

_____

Conclusion

The major points were summarized	4 3 2 1
Time was allowed for questions or discussion	4 3 2 1
There was a feeling of "closure" to the presentation	4 3 2 1

What was the single greatest strength demonstrated by the facilitator in this lecture/presentation?

What would make this facilitation stronger or more effective?

Chapter 9:
Planning for Group Discussion

In some ways we can argue that this chapter and the next one are the most important chapters in this book. The reason for our making such an assertion is that group discussion, more than any other "technique" in teaching, expresses the true values of adult education. If adult education means student-centered learning, developing a spirit of educational democracy, honoring pluralism and difference, and providing opportunities for the expression of individual voices, it is hard to imagine a more opportune place to exercise these values than in a classroom discussion.

That being said, we must also confess that discussion facilitation is the most challenging aspect of teaching. Because no two groups of learners are ever the same, nor are any two adult education situations exactly alike, every group discussion facilitation is unique. It is possible to imagine a well-prepared lecture working nicely again and again over time with different groups of learners (although, as we have discussed, if there is ample dialogue built into the lecture there will be differences between experiences here, too). But it is not possible to even imagine two group discussions being alike. This is one of many reasons why, even after 30 years of combined experience teaching adults, we believe that planning (this chapter) and facilitating (the next chapter) successful discussions remain our greatest challenge. And when it works well, this experience yields our greatest reward in teaching.

Why Bother?

The well-known adult educator and writer, Stephen Brookfield, in his recent book *Discussion as a Way of Teaching* (co-authored with Stephen Preskill), lists numerous reasons why discussions matter. Let's briefly explore some of these reasons.

Discussion takes place in all types of adult education environments. In other words, classroom discussions are as close to universal as any educational methodology. Even in a course that is dominated by lecture or presentation, discussion still occurs (although it may not be as fluid and open as discussions we shall advocate for in this and the next chapter). In courses that are heavily slanted toward laboratory work or hands-on "studio" activities, there will nonetheless be discussion between the teacher and students and among students themselves. So the first response to "Why bother?" is that discussion of one sort or other will always have a place in an adult education environment.

Discussion helps students become connected. Building connections, both personal and intellectual, are among the most important outcomes of participating in adult education. And making connections is at the very heart of group discussion. Ideas that may seem distant or irrelevant when presented through a lecture often come alive when we have a chance to talk about them and relate them to our own experiences. And classmates who sit passively next to us during a film or presentation become interesting and engaging human beings when we speak and listen to their stories and ideas. Group discussions are often the best bridge available in the adult education classroom to lead students from disconnection and isolation to an experience of meaning-making and belonging.

Classroom discussion helps students explore a diversity of perspectives. While teachers can always introduce diverse perspectives on an issue through lectures, reading assignments, films, etc., there is nothing quite like students' hearing from each other's lips the multiple interpretations that can be made of the same apparently objective facts. People find it less convenient to ignore a contrary view expressed by a peer than to skip a few paragraphs in a book or "tune out" parts of a lecture. Of course, the more diverse the group itself (with regard to gender, race, politics, age, and levels of experience with the subject at hand) the greater will be the diversity of points of view.

Discussion increases students' awareness of and tolerance for ambiguity. A good discussion is one that leaves issues open for further inquiry and in which as many questions are raised as are answered. In successful discussions people learn that the ideas they brought with them to the class are limited and that the topic being explored is far more complex than earlier believed. For this reason we feel strongly that group discussion is not a good tool when it is your intention to initiate students into a predefined body of truths or facts. There are many other ways described in this book to accomplish that goal. However, group discussion is an outstanding method if the goal is to expand horizons of thinking, help people to grow in appreciation of the richness and complexity of a subject, or honestly generate a sense of wonder that can stimulate further desire to learn.

Discussion helps people to examine their assumptions. Few of us are able to examine critically our assumptions on our own. This hard and important work—which is the best road to deep and transformational learning—almost always comes through dialogue with others. In group discussion students can serve as critical mirrors for each other, reflecting the assumptions they see in each other's positions. They can question one another about what is said in the group and why it was said (or said "that way"). We learn to think differently by way of receiving feedback about how we are thinking right now. While the teacher has a role to play in giving such feedback, in an adult education environment, peer learners play at least as great—if not greater—role.

Discussion encourages attentive and respectful listening. For the most part our society does not honor listening. Instead, we tend to give praise to well-spoken words (the "first rank" in a class of students is the valedictorian, which literally means one who speaks well). But in a well-facilitated class discussion, listening is extremely important. In fact, not much good happens without it. Think about it—if there are 10 people in the group and one person at a time is speaking, 90% of the "action" lies in listening. But listening with care and attention is not easy. It requires practice. The adult education classroom is an excellent place for all learners—students and teachers alike—to develop the skill of attentive and respectful listening. And it is worth the investment of time in class to commit to this practice because many of the larger goals to which adult education aspires—developing a sense of personal empowerment, confidence, and voice—will derive from the experience of being listened to well.

Discussion enables learners to become teachers and teachers to continue to be learners. In discussion (or at least the "best" of class discussions), students and teachers share the space and the power. Students' ideas have as much right to be examined and adopted as the facilitator's. It is an empowering experience when a student expresses an opinion or shares an experience that moves the group to a new place of understanding and appreciation. It has been said that if a stranger walked into an adult education discussion, she or he would not be able to tell the teacher from the students. This is because in a well-managed group discussion everyone is a teacher and everyone is a learner.

Setting the Context

A stimulating discussion is, paradoxically, both well-planned and spontaneous. The "magic" of a good discussion is often serendipitous, but the magic does not take place if proper preparations have not been made.

One of the most important aspects of preparation has to do with the group itself. It is hard, if not impossible, to facilitate discussion among people who do not know or trust each other very well. People will not take the risk of sharing their ideas or opinions if a basic sense of trust in one's fellow learners and you the teacher has not been established. We have already discussed how to plan an icebreaker activity or other method of "warming up" the people in the class. It is important to do this before trying to engage a class discussion. In fact, it may be best to wait until at least the second or third class in the semester before you try having a group discussion. This will allow time for people in the class to get to know and develop trust in one another.

Another planning element is to keep in mind the purpose of the discussion. Is it to explore some issue that is truly open ended and has no single answer? Is it to see what people know about a topic or question? Is it to express points of view about a subject the class is struggling to understand? Will the discussion be used to debrief a lecture or film? Is it to formulate arguments and counter-arguments about a position? Is it to try to get the class to solve a problem (hypothetical or actual)? All of these are sound purposes for having a group discussion. But if the purpose is unclear—to you and to your students—there is a greater chance that the discussion will not be a satisfactory experience. Some class discussions feel like they are "spinning wheels" because its purpose has never been thought through by the teacher and expressed to the class.

It is also sound teaching practice to help students prepare for an upcoming discussion. Elsewhere in this book we have written about advance-organizers. This is a powerful tool for helping students become prepared for discussion. Assigning a specific reading, handing out discussion questions in advance, posing a problem to be considered ahead of time, or inviting students to bring their own questions for discussion will often greatly enhance the quality of the dialogue. Again that paradox: it takes careful preparation and planning—on the part of both you and your students—to ultimately experience a rich and rewarding spontaneity in group discussion.

The physical environment is also important. It is nearly impossible to have a fluid and balanced discussion if students are seated in straight lines or rows. Some classrooms do not lend themselves well to discussion either because the furniture is not movable or they are too small to create a circle or square (a circle is best because everyone can see everyone else; but having tables arranged in a square or rectangle is better than in straight lines). We have sometimes chosen to move our class to another environment for the sake of setting a better context for discussion. Talking with the adult education director or building administrator in advance about having an alternative site for group discussion may be a worthwhile strategy. Sometimes school buildings have a teachers' lounge, conference room, or some other suitable facility available at night that will be more conducive to establishing a suitable context for an adult education discussion group than your regular classroom.

Establish Discussion Ground Rules

Rules of conduct are important in group discussions. Without a code of behavior there is a risk that students will not take the discussion as seriously as you'd like or that the conversation will quickly degenerate into a "free-for-all." Ground rules help to structure the process in order to ensure the discussion is democratic, civil, and purposeful.

There are two primary ways of establishing ground rules. As the teacher you may choose to set these rules, perhaps even typing them out on a piece of paper as a handout or, in the least, listing them on a flip chart. An example of a simple set of ground rules is as follows:

- Everyone participates at least once during the discussion
- There is no such thing as a "stupid" question or idea
- Limit each contribution to no more than two minutes
- One person talks at a time
- Listen to and respect other people's ideas even if you do not agree with them

Ground rules can become more complex as the group grows together in experience. For example, you may wish to add an item such as "Try not to let your previous ideas or prejudices interfere with hearing another point of view," or "Work to provide encouragement and approval," or even "Seek out differences of opinion because they will enrich the discussion."

The second way to formulate a conduct code for a class discussion is to allow your students to do it. As the teacher you could facilitate a brainstorming process before the initial group discussion that evokes the kinds of ground rules your students want to live with for the rest of the course. These could be voted on or otherwise adopted by the group. Brookfield and Preskill suggest a process for eliciting student input that is based on a critical incident method of collecting information. They begin by asking their students to think of the best group discussion each person has ever experienced. What happened in that discussion that made the conversation so satisfying? Now think of an especially awful discussion experience. What made it so bad? The class then breaks into small groups and shares these incidents. They seek common themes. Finally, the large group comes back together, explores what has been learned in the smaller groups about good and bad class discussions, and works to create a class "charter." This charter becomes the ground rules the class agrees to abide by for the rest of the semester. This second alternative is more difficult to manage and assumes both a high degree of commitment and maturity on the part of the students participating in the process. However, it is a marvelous example of learner-centered adult education in practice.

Getting Started

Once you have thought about the purpose of discussion in the larger context of your class and have made preparations to set the context, it is time to begin the facilitation. *Any one* of the following suggestions might make for a good starting point. As you continue to teach and—we hope—use group discussion as a mode of facilitating adult learning, over time you may wish to try several of these strategies for getting started.

Refer to the advance-organizer. This is a good place to start, because you assume people have spent some time thinking about and otherwise preparing the advance-organizer you prepared and distributed earlier (this may have been handed out in the previous class, communicated via e-mail, etc.). In fact, if you did not refer to the advance-organizer either at the beginning or sometime during the body of the discussion, you would jeopardize your students' trust and willingness to prepare the next time.

Ask for students' questions. This actually could be part of an advance-organizer, e.g., specifically asking people to bring one or more questions with them to the next class. But if you have not requested this in advance, spending time at the beginning of a class discussion generating questions about a specific idea/book/film/assignment—and listing those questions on the board or flip chart—may be an excellent starting point for dialogue.

Begin with a truly "open" question. As compared with a so-called "closed" question that typically has a specified and known answer (e.g., What colors are on the national flag of Italy? What is the square root of 81?), "open" questions do not have a pre-determined answer and hence may lead the discussion in a wide variety of directions. Examples of open questions are "How would you describe the author's voice in this story?," "What feelings were evoked by this piece of music we just heard?," and "Why did so few Germans oppose Adolf Hitler in the 1930s?" A good open question will often generate students' interest. Almost any question, based on the reading assignment or something your students have in common, will do. A mistake some teachers make is that they try to generate discussion with questions that are not particularly open or stimulating. Also, if you asked a series of questions to which the answers are already known (by you), you risk making the conversation feel like a fishing expedition. Or worse—like an oral examination. If your students begin to feel they are being quizzed in a discussion, their enthusiasm will quickly shut down. So if you are working on a biology unit, instead of asking your class,

"What is a cell?," try something like "Please describe one or two characteristics of cells that you find most interesting." Instead of asking, "What is the definition of software," try "When you think of software, what images come to mind?"

Start the discussion with a "Minute Paper." Yes—here is another good use for this simple writing technique. This will work especially well if there has not been a specific advance-organizer prepared for the discussion. Ask students to take out a blank piece of paper and write for two (or three) minutes about the question or issue you will be discussing as a group. Some students will feel more ready to join a discussion if they have had even a few minutes to organize their thoughts. After students have finished writing, ask for volunteers to read their "Minute Paper." Conversation can flow from those stimuli.

Use journal prompts. If you use journal writing as a tool in your course, it may be a good idea every once in a while to begin a class discussion with a journal prompt. For example, in a job readiness course have students take a few minutes of class time to write a response to the following prompt: "Describe a problem you encountered at work and the steps you took to resolve it." Then ask for several volunteers to read their journal entry.

Pose questions based on a shared experience. A shared experience—a field trip, film, demonstration, recent lecture—can stimulate an exchange that reveals students' different perceptions and reactions to the same event. One of the paths the discussion may take is to explore how and why people had such differing perspectives on the same experience.

Make a controversial statement. Surprise and uncertainty arouses curiosity. If you want to get people excited (and perhaps even angry), make a bold claim and then ask for responses: "The Social Security System is a failure and should be promptly shut down!" "We should have a law banning T.V. all but three hours per day!" "After the 2000 election it is clear that we need a new constitutional amendment to elect the president by popular rather than electoral vote!" Statements such as these can be formulated in just about any subject area. While there can be no guarantees, the chances are good that a dynamic discussion will ensue from such a startling start.

Begin with small groups. Sub-groupings of the entire class—sometimes called "buzz groups"—will provide a more comfortable setting for a number of learners. Many people find it easier to share thoughts and feelings with three or four classmates than with fifteen, twenty, or twenty-five. You can manage the divisions by having students count off, by clustering people by where they are sitting, or by some other means. We talk more about assigning members of small groups specific tasks in the chapter on Cooperative Learning. Any of the stimuli for beginning a class discussion that we are enumerating here will work with small groups as well as an at-large class discussion. In almost every case you will want to convene the entire class together after the buzz groups in order to debrief the experience and allow students to learn from each others' small group experiences.

Tell a story. Storytelling is perhaps the most primordial way human beings have taught and learned from one another. Much of the great literature we have inherited from ancient times—the *Odyssey*, the *Iliad*, the *Bible*—is based on stories. Telling a story is also a powerful way to evoke thoughts and feelings in others. The story you tell may be based on fact or fiction, but try to make it connect to some point you are treating in the course. After you tell the story there are numerous ways the discussion might begin: What do you think? What are your feelings upon hearing this story? If there was a sequel to this story what might happen next? What does this story mean to you? Among the best stories we teachers can tell are autobiographical ones, e.g., those that relate to a part of our own lives. Students are interested in us as people. By sharing a story from our own experience we set a tone and encourage our students to share their own stories. Conversations deepen and become more trusting when human stories are shared in an adult education classroom.

Facilitating the Discussion

Once the discussion has begun it is time to enjoy the ride. Your job is to listen, respond appropriately to students' comments, intervene if the group hits a road block (in either the process or content of the discussion), and tweak the conversation here and there to ensure that you are meeting your goals.

The entire next chapter is designed to help you think about and manage problems that commonly arise in facilitating a class discussion. Assuredly, in nearly every situation you face, there will be something to manage. There has never been—nor will there ever be—the "perfect discussion." By paying attention to some of the issues that commonly arise in facilitating group discussion you will grow to appreciate and use what Eduard Lindeman, Malcolm Knowles, Stephen Brookfield, and thousands of other adult educators (including the two of us) believe to be the supreme method of teaching adults. And in nearly every case you and your students will indeed enjoy the ride.

Chapter 10:
Facilitating Group Discussions

The previous chapter helped you to think about why discussions are important in adult education and how to begin a discussion with your class. This chapter deals mostly with the practical aspects of actually leading discussions.

One metaphor we like for teaching generally, but that seems to work even better as a way of describing the facilitation of a group discussion, is that of the orchestra conductor. The role of a conductor is obviously important. she or he keeps the musicians together, sets the pace and volume of the music, and generally manages the activity. But the conductor does not actually make any music—the violinists, clarinet players, cellists, trumpeters, and other players do. Together they work as a team, and when things go well an orchestra makes beautiful music. An energetic, thoughtful, and balanced adult education discussion is no less a work of art.

Your main role as a group discussion leader is to prepare sound conditions for the activity (this is the main message of the previous chapter) and then let your students loose to make their music. Once the discussion has begun most of your attention is paid to managing the pace, rhythm, and direction of the conversation and if necessary "tweaking" things so everyone has a voice and learning is maximized. The subtleties of group discussions are enormous and, unlike a lecture, many variables are out of your control. To continue the conducting metaphor, you really don't have influence over whether or not the flutist is playing the right notes! But you may be able to manage the amplification of the flutist and the other musicians so the orchestra as a whole still achieves its goal of making pleasing music.

We have designed this chapter as a problem-solving primer for the new teacher of adults who wishes to facilitate discussions. Many situations will occur in discussion facilitation—among new and even highly experienced facilitators—that will require intervention. Please read each situation below and, before reading the possible solutions we provide, think about what you would do if this particular circumstance occurred in your class. By the end of this chapter we hope you will have a broader set of ideas to use as resources when these situations arise in discussion groups (rest assured, many of them will). We also hope that thinking about these situations and their potential solutions will help you to build confidence to assume the challenge of conducting a group discussion.

The New Teacher of Adults

Situation #1:

One or two people in the class are clearly dominating the discussion. Other voices have been stifled by these aggressive participants.

What would you do? _____

_____

_____

_____

_____

_____

_____

This is among the most common problems that arise in discussions. We suggest several possible solutions. First, you might try to withdraw your eye contact from the dominating people. Students will look to the facilitator for approval, and if they see that you have averted your attention away from them it may signal that you are not pleased with their continued aggressive posture in the group. You may also want to raise the issue in a direct manner to the class, saying something like: "We have heard from several people on this issue. What do others of you think?" Another direct approach might be: "Would this discussion be better if more people were participating?" We know of teachers who, when continually faced with this problem, assign a small sub-group to be observers. Their job is to watch the group dynamics and then report back to the class. Hearing from peers that one or two members of the class are clearly dominating the conversation may help to solve the problem. A variation on this approach is to audio or videotape a section of a discussion and then play it back for everyone to hear and/or see, asking people to comment on levels of participation, balance, etc. Finally, in some cases we find that the approach that works the best is to address this issue privately with the offending people. In most cases we want to balance confrontation with a degree of support and encouragement (e.g, "You are making some valuable contributions to the class discussion") because we do not want these people to withdraw entirely from future conversations.

Situation #2:

The discussion seems to be wandering aimlessly.

What would you do? _____

_____

_____

_____

_____

_____

_____

_____

_____

_____

We wrote earlier about the importance of having goal(s) for the discussion. This may be a good time to re-state what the discussion was intended to achieve. So "re-focusing" may be a key task for you if such a situation occurred. You may also wish to throw the issue back to the group by saying something like: "Has anyone noticed that we seem to have wandered pretty far away from where we began this discussion?" or "We seem to have gone off on a tangent. Would somebody like to help us get back on track?" Students will be more than happy to help re-focus the discussion if they share your view that the dialogue has wandered off into unproductive territory.

Situation #3:

You are asking questions, but nobody is responding.

What would you do? _____

_____

_____

_____

_____

_____

_____

_____

_____

_____

First, it is important not to react too quickly to this situation. It may be a case where people need adequate response time and patience on your part is the remedy. However, once you have patiently waited for responses to your questions and there are still long silences, the problem(s) lie elsewhere. And again, as with each of these common problems that arise in discussions, there are a number of possible remedies. You might ask the class, "What's going on? Nobody seems to have anything to say today." You may also stop and look at the kinds of questions you have been asking. Are they threatening? Are they unclear? Are they so close-ended that they feel like you are giving an oral quiz? Threatening, unclear, or closed questions may easily silence students. Or, does the problem lie in poor preparation? Perhaps your students were not clear about the assignment that was intended to prepare them for this discussion. If you asked them, they will probably tell you if they were confused about how they were expected to prepare.

Situation #4:

There is a good deal more on the agenda to accomplish for tonight's class and time is close to running out.

What would you do? _____

_____

_____

_____

_____

_____

In some cases this situation has a bright side. One of the reasons we may run out of time in a discussion is because the conversation has developed nicely, many (or all) members of the class have participated, and there has been a genuinely positive flow of energy in the group. However, one potential victim of this success is not quite getting all the things accomplished that you had set out to do in this session. What to do? Several options present themselves. First, you may simply let go of some of the agenda. Is everything we targeted to accomplish tonight really necessary? Or—if not let go of items altogether—can one or two be deferred until the next class? Or can they be handled outside of class by way of a reading or writing activity or perhaps a parallel conversation on an electronic discussion board? In the spirit of adult education you might, upon recognizing that everything on the agenda will not get done, ask the group to take a few minutes to help prioritize the remaining activities. It is important to consider the fact that the teaching-learning contract is organic in nature and may change depending on circumstances. In any event, one thing we would strongly advise that you not do in this situation is to rush all of the unfinished business into the remaining time. This "Blitzkrieg" approach will most likely cheapen the curriculum and will almost assuredly frustrate your students. And, especially if this problem arose in the first place as a result of having an especially good flow of discussion during the first part of class, it would be unfortunate to follow a healthy and presumably rich learning experience with a rushed and shallow one.

Situation #5:

The group has achieved a reasonable consensus in the discussion of an issue, but there are several strong dissenters.

What would you do? _____

_____

_____

_____

_____

_____

_____

_____

Several possibilities present themselves. You could summarize both viewpoints at the end of the discussion and seek the group's agreement that these in fact are the key ideas that have emerged from the discussion process. There is no problem with leaving it right there ("Agreement" is not necessarily a goal of discussions while exploration and learning are. In fact, dissension is often a natural outcome of a safe learning environment that encourages democratic discourse). Another possible response would be to ask members of each of the opposing positions to take a few minutes in a buzz group to summarize the other position and report back to the entire class. This strategy would force each side to show that they have listened and have achieved a reasonable understanding of the opposing position. You may wish to use a variation on this idea by facilitating a "two column" posting on the black board or flip chart. You can ask each side to list the key ideas in support of the other sides' position. In any event, what is most important is that this experience does not become overly competitive or antagonistic. Usually there are two sides (at least) to an issue and the outcome of a wholesome adult education discussion will be for learners to develop a more thoughtful appreciation of both sides.

Situation #6:

Two members of the class do not like each other. At times they are actually antagonistic toward each other, which affects the entire nature of the group discussion.

What would you do? _____

_____

_____

_____

_____

_____

_____

_____

_____

This is a tough one. It has the potential for casting a toxic spell over the entire class. Unfortunately this situation does occur, albeit, thankfully, not with a great deal of frequency. During the times when such person-to-person antagonism has become an issue in our classes, we have chosen to deal with it directly outside of class. Seeking an appointment with each party separately may be the best place to begin. Confronting each individual with the reality that their vitriol is hurting the entire class dynamic often results in the damaging behavior ameliorating or disappearing altogether. If necessary the separate one-on-one meetings could lead to a session with you and the two antagonists to talk the matter through. A more public way of dealing with this problem that involves the entire group is to turn this situation into an opportunity to establish a clear set of ground rules for discussions. If ground rules have already been established and this situation still occurs, either those rules have not been followed or they are in need of expansion (to include items such as "civility" toward all members of the group).

Situation #7:

It is apparent that people have not done their homework. Lack of preparation is bringing about a lackluster discussion.

What would you do? _____

_____

_____

_____

_____

_____

_____

All kinds of issues emerge here. Did something happen in the world at large that preoccupied your students during the past week and kept them away from their studies? Obvious examples would be a war, natural disaster, or some major public event that captures headlines. Or, is something else going on with the class itself? Are most people discouraged or feeling lost? Have they "given up" on this particular unit of study? Still another possibility is that you have been too much in control of discussions in the past and students feel they can get away without being prepared because you'll end up talking most of the time anyway. McKeachie reports that in a typical discussion (his sample was in college classrooms) the teacher actually talked 70–80 percent of the time! If that has been the pattern in your class up until now, and you suddenly decide to shift the focus and expect substantial student participation, your students may not be ready to take on this role. Once again, you could take a direct approach and say something like the following: "I've noticed that you don't seem prepared today. What's going on?" A variation on this might be: "It seems as though few, if any, of you are prepared to talk about _____ today. So, what are you prepared to talk about?" This question may get to some valuable insights about the course itself, what is working and not working for your students, etc. Remember—this is your students' course. They own the learning. If most students have not done their homework in a specific unit of study, the problem might lie in that unit rather than in other easy-to-make judgments (concerning their laziness, having a bad day, etc.).

Situation #8:

You observe the appearance of bewilderment in the faces of several of your students.

What would you do? _____

_____

_____

_____

_____

_____

_____

_____

_____

_____

_____

First, it needs to be said that bewilderment may not be all that bad. Sometimes we have to experience confusion before clarity emerges. "The disorderliness of discovery" is often an important stage in the learning process. And there can be a certain tyranny to too much tidiness. That being said, perhaps this is still another time to mirror your perception back to the group: "I've noticed that a number of you look somewhat bewildered right now. May I ask you what you're thinking or feeling?" This may be an excellent point at which to ask people to write a "Minute Paper" summarizing their understanding of the main idea you have been treating in class or even their thoughts and/or feelings right now at this moment in the class. Discussion facilitation requires patience. Things will not always be easy and clear. While deeper understanding is, in most cases, a desired long-term goal of discussion, the process that gets you there may take students through bewilderment, confusion, and a cacophony of other uncomfortable conditions.

Situation #9:

A student's feelings are hurt by a sharp comment made by another member of the group.

What would you do? _____

_____

_____

_____

_____

_____

_____

_____

_____

One thing that immediately needs to be assessed here is whether the sharp comment was aimed at the student's idea(s) or her/his person. If the latter, the attacking behavior must be stopped and an apology by the offending party made. There is no room in a democratic and presumably civil discussion for personal attacks. It is hard to imagine that even the most liberal set of ground rules would allow for such personal attacks.

Errors in thinking, however, are an integral part of education. Most people will get things wrong before they get them right. And pointing out erroneous thinking is the job of both students and the teacher. It is possible, albeit not always easy, to find something useful even in a flawed statement. You want to be encouraging without allowing the erroneous idea to remain alive.

Deeply hurt feelings may require a private conversation with the concerned parties in order to work the problem through. The aggrieved student will need to feel supported by you. Time spent outside of class on behalf of mediating this kind of difficulty is usually well-invested. Please remember that many students have low self-esteem and will not venture forth into a group discussion again if they feel put down by classmates and not supported by the teacher. Rejection or ridicule will silence a person quickly. It will likely even cause her/him to quit the course. So, once again, this is a place to take care. That being said, it's possible to take still another slant on this issue. In an essay about ethics in discussion groups, David Garvin wrote: "Many students would be better off if they were treated less delicately. The ability to survive public criticism, after all, is an important professional skill and one that must be learned. Often, a supportive classroom is the best environment for such lessons. Providing *ad hominem* attacks are to be avoided and fellow students aim to be helpful, even weak students should be capable of rising above their mistakes. For many of them, the fear of error is likely to be worse than the reality . . . " (Garvin in Christensen, et. al., p. 296). The specific student(s) involved and the context in which situation #9 occurs will greatly determine your most appropriate response as a teacher.

Situation #10:

The group, working hard to build a sense of community, appears afraid to be critical. Every idea that is expressed, even shallow ones, is approved and even praised.

What would you do? _____

_____

_____

_____

_____

_____

_____

_____

_____

_____

This situation is closely related to #9. In a healthy adult education discussion you want to have both a spirit of encouragement and criticism. Most people have a difficult time giving constructive criticism, and we believe the teacher must role model this behavior. There are several approaches we support. One is the "Yes, Yes, But . . . " model. What this means is that before you point to the mistake in the argument, comment about two good things you have heard. For example: "Jane—It is clear to me that you have spent a lot of time reading our course materials in preparation for this discussion. I like the passion you have for Mr. Smith's writing. However, have you considered that Smith was writing fiction here and that this is not a true story."

Another, albeit similar, approach is what is sometimes called the "Oreo Cookie" model. That is, sandwich a critical comment between two positive ones. Again, let's focus on Jane. "You made some excellent points about the main characters in this story Jane. I have serious reservations, however, about your judgment that the protagonist was mentally ill. In my view you are on track with your other thoughts, however."

Still another approach to this problem is—once again—to throw it back on the group. "We seem to have difficulty giving constructive criticism to one another." This will provide the class with an opportunity to talk about ways to make criticism work more effectively in the context of this course. Because giving effective feedback is such an important, difficult, and challenging thing, asking students to explore this matter may result in some of the most useful learning they achieve in your class.

Situation #11:

Lots of questions are being asked by students, but they are directed exclusively at you. Therefore, what had been planned as a group discussion has degenerated into a "Q and A" session.

What would you do? _____

_____

_____

_____

_____

_____

_____

_____

_____

_____

You probably have begun to see a pattern here. Certain responses work well in a variety of situations. So once again you may choose to name the problem as you have diagnosed it, saying to your students: "Perhaps you have noticed that over the past ten minutes our discussion has transformed into a question and answer session." Ask them (1) if they agree with this diagnosis and (2) if they do, how they would like to handle it? Another possible remedy would be to begin to answer a student's question with another question. This would help to break up the habitual question-answer-question-answer cycle.

Situation #12:

Describe a problem that you have encountered with a group discussion that is at least somewhat different than the eleven we have listed in this chapter. This problem could be one that arose in a class you took as a student, in a work situation, or somewhere else.

What did the teacher (or group leader) do at the time? _____

_____

_____

_____

_____

_____

_____

What would you do now? _____

_____

_____

_____

_____

_____

We hope it is clear from this chapter that discussions are inherently uncertain. There are so many intricacies and variables operating simultaneously that it is indeed a challenging task to assume the "conductor's role" as a discussion facilitator. But also please remember that there has never been and there never will be the "perfect" discussion (some wise person once said that none of us has enough time to seek perfection). Despite the risks, we believe discussion groups represent the supreme method of adult education. It is democratic learning at its best. We wholeheartedly encourage you to try facilitating group discussions as part of your teaching practice.

Chapter 11:
Teaching through Writing

We have learned over the years that most students divide into one of two camps: those who enjoy and those who hate to write. But both of these kinds of learners—in the end—will come around to admitting that writing often can lead them to some of the deepest and best learning they encounter throughout their educational experience.

Why does writing facilitate learning? Skill in thinking is similar to skill in music or athletics. It takes practice to improve. Much of our thinking remains in our minds unless it is put on paper. We force ourselves to clarify our thoughts by expressing them. A character in one of E.M. Forster's novels put it this way: "How do I know what I think until I see what I say?" Writing helps us to "see" what we are thinking. And then, if our writing is shared with a teacher or—as sometimes may be the case—with classmates or colleagues, other people also get to see what we are thinking and can provide helpful feedback.

Most of us who teach adults were not English majors in college or enthusiastic writers in high school. We may be uncertain of some of the rules of grammar and syntax. We may even have doubts about our own abilities to write well (this is a common sentiment among even highly educated professionals). But we can still encourage our students to write and reinforce the fact that writing is a tried and true way of learning.

"Low Stakes" Writing

Writing that does not count for a grade is sometimes referred to as "low stakes." In other words, the pressure is off. This more relaxed writing may be done in class or on one's own time outside of a formal educational environment. The "minute paper" that we describe elsewhere in this book is a good example of low stakes writing. In most cases these brief, summary-like papers are not even collected by the teacher. And if they are, the reason for reading them is for you to learn what people are thinking at a particular moment in the course.

One popular form of low stakes writing is the journal or diary (while some people note technical differences between a journal and a diary, we prefer to use these terms synonymously). In our own teaching practice we frequently and enthusiastically encourage students to write journal entries about what they are learning. They may do so using a bound diary-like book, on regular pads of 8 ½" x 11" lined or blank paper, or with their computer. Learning journals may consist of reactions to course readings, thoughts in response to a class presentation or lecture, feelings about the subject matter encountered at various points in the course, questions posed by the teacher, or even the student's reaction to participating in an adult education experience in the first place.

Journals can often set an agenda for future learning by listing unanswered questions of interest that have arisen that will require further thinking and reading and/or discussion. They can act as a reflective learning tool. There are times when a substantial journal entry might primarily constitute a simple list. Such a list might be based on any of the following questions:

- What are the five most important things I learned in class today?
- How might I state the "big ideas" I derived from this book chapter I have just read?
- What are my feelings about this course as a whole? And—after each statement of feeling—why do I feel this way?
- In what practical way(s) might I be able to apply what I learned in tonight's class to my work and family life?
- After tonight's class (or this article I just read, or this book . . .), what questions do I have now about the subject matter I am studying?

Journal entries can be used for topics related to learning autobiographies. Learning autobiographies help students critically reflect on prior learning experiences. For example, math autobiographical journal prompts might include such questions as:

- How do you feel about your prior math experiences?
- What have been your experiences with math teachers?

- Is there a time when you liked math? Hated it? Why do you feel the way you do?
- Do you have any special strategies for getting through math classes?

Please refer to Exhibit 11-2 for an example of a detailed set of writing prompts used in one adult education mathematics course. Another example comes from a course in "Job Readiness:"

- Everybody has difficult moments at work. How did you handle conflict with a fellow worker, supervisor? Be specific.
- How would a former supervisor describe you?
- What are your long-range goals?
- How well do you work under pressure? Can you give an example of how you handled stress in the workplace?

However, it is important to note that learning journals are only low stakes if they are not collected, read, and evaluated. There are some exceptions (e.g., Job Readiness) that involve open discussion of journal questions because they are directly related to other critical applications such as interview questions or other activities. In general, we believe student writing that is as intimate and personal as a journal should not be formally graded. There are too many dicey issues that arise when journal entries themselves become the basis of evaluation (e.g., Is there an undercurrent of meaning that the greater the personal risk taken in journal writing, the better the grade? If so, what are the implications of this assumption with regard to the potential abuse of power between teacher and student? Will students be honest if they know everything they write will be read by somebody else?).

Admittedly there are teachers who do read their students' actual (original) journal entries, dialogue with these journals, and achieve success. In such cases parameters for the writing and responding have been established and the students feel safe sharing even highly personal reflections. But we believe this is a riskier situation than the one that we present below.

If you wish to encourage journal writing, and also want to ensure that students appreciate the fact that their journals count in some important way in the work of the course, you may want to ask for what we call "journal summaries." A journal summary is what it sounds like—an overview of the major ideas that have originally been articulated in journal entries. Writing a summary provides an opportunity for students to look back over their original journal entries (composed over the past week, two weeks, or whatever time frame you have agreed to), select key themes that have emerged, and write a summary of these ideas that will be turned in, read, discussed, and possibly evaluated. This procedure protects the confidentiality of the original entries, yet allows the student nonetheless to experience the salutary effects of journal writing and also of "mining" the original entries for the largest nuggets of gold that are there. By the way, it is very important that if you decide to adopt this procedure and "count" journal summaries as part of a formal evaluation that you are clear as to the criteria that will be used. We say more about this a bit later in this chapter.

Before we leave journal writing, there is one other situation that you may encounter and have to deal with when you give your students the opportunity to write about private aspects of their lives. Stories may arise that deal with past or current abuse. There may be thoughts expressed about depression and suicide. Or you may otherwise read a "cry for help" a student's narrative. If you encounter these or a related situation it would be wise to go to your program director and ask about local mental health services to which you might refer your student. In some rare cases writing about a difficult situation can precipitate an emotional crisis. Having a list of referral sources available will facilitate your helping your student. It is also important to note that in cases where domestic violence and/or child abuse are suspected, many states have laws governing disclosure. Again, your program director will be an important source of information and support should you encounter such incidents in your teaching.

While, as we have just discussed, so-called "low stakes" writing on rare occasions can become high stakes emotionally, there are other options for writing activities in the adult education classroom where grading or formal evaluation is not an issue (often because the course does not carry academic credit). The encouragement of writing in these situations is based on the learning opportunities the act of writing itself presents.

One simple and time-tested form of writing is the "personal letter." There are times when we have students write letters to each other. These can be useful in order to provide feedback about an in-class presentation or a project a classmate is working on. There are times when we have asked students to write to a friend or family member. In one course on the subject of aging, an assignment was to summarize the best ideas learned throughout the semester and write a letter to an older person you know. People chose a grandparent, parent, an elder aunt or uncle, and in some cases a long-time friend or neighbor. The feedback received about this activity was that it yielded multiple gains. Students met the challenge of organizing numerous ideas into a relatively brief and coherent narrative (it was suggested that they take their time with this activity and write a reasonably brief but thoughtful letter—based on Rainer Rilke's observation to a friend that he would have written a shorter letter if he had had more time!). The recipient of the correspondence benefited from both the content of the letter and the act of communicating itself. Several students brought back the news that their letter was going to be kept by their older relative or friend as a treasured artifact. This is how powerful such a personal communication can be.

Another letter writing idea may be to have students write the editor of the local newspaper or to their State Representative or member of U.S. Congress. This activity has the added potential benefit of influencing change in an important area of policy. It also engages people in the democratic process. Still another application would be to have students compose a book review in the form of a letter to the author of the book(s) you are using in your class (you and your students can decide whether these letters will actually be mailed or remain unsent). A technique that perhaps gets a little on the wild side yet could nonetheless be both fun and productive is to have students write a letter to a famous dead person. In a physics class write to Albert Einstein or in a religion class write to Moses or St. Paul.

I hope we have gotten the message across that there are an infinite variety of ways for teachers to use creatively the age-old practice of letter writing to a positive effect in adult education.

Writing That Counts for a Grade

Grading students' writing is one of the most challenging aspects of teaching (please also see the chapter on assessment). It is important to remember that the learning will occur from the activity of thinking and writing and the substantive feedback you give to the ideas that are expressed in your students' paper. The grade itself—while important—will not yield learning.

If the context of your course of study requires that student writing be formally evaluated/graded, it is only fair that each person has a clear indication of the criteria that will be used. These criteria should be set forth in the course syllabus and perhaps even in a special handout that is given out later in the course as a reminder. In some instances the criteria may be written clearly on the black/white board or a flip chart.

Wilbert McKeachie, in his book *Teaching Tips,* provides a detailed example of such a statement of criteria for a term paper. While he intended these guidelines for a college-level paper, you may find much of this list useful for your purposes in public school adult education.

A. Content of the Paper
- Does the writer clearly state the purpose, problem, or question to be considered?
- Is the presentation of arguments, including evidence to support the arguments, clear and logical?
- Are multiple sources considered if available?
- Is the writing well-organized and easy to comprehend?
- In the body of the paper does the author treat the problem or issue that is posed at the beginning?
- Does the author provide an appropriate summary of her/his ideas?
- Is the conclusion plausible and does it relate to the main arguments in the paper?

B. Connections to the Class
- Is there evidence that class materials have been read and understood?

- Has there been an application of lecture materials, class discussions, and assigned readings to the paper?

C. Form
- Is the paper written with the use of good spelling and grammar?
- Paragraph form: Are ideas presented in coherent order?
- Footnotes and bibliography: Are borrowed ideas and statements given credit? Is the form of the footnotes and bibliography understandable and consistent?

It is a matter of fairness that students know the criteria for grading well in advance of writing their paper. In the case where detailed criteria such as those listed above are used, it is advised that samples of exemplary work be made available to the student. If there is an adequate photocopying budget these exemplars could be printed and given to each member of the class. In the least they should be made available in a file that is easily accessible (in the library, a resource room, or adult education director's office).

One excellent adult education tool that honors the maturity and integrity of the learner is to allow for self-evaluation of writing. This self-evaluation could count for a portion or even the entirety of the paper's grade. The criteria for success are known and may even have been co-determined by the learners themselves (this represents another excellent tradition in adult education). We believe the learner is in as good a position as anyone to assess how well she or he has met the agreed-upon standard. The self-evaluation report may be expressed by way of a memo, letter, or simple checklist.

Another way to evaluate writing is to engage peer review. Asking students to read and comment upon each other's written work—while risky—demonstrates substantial trust in their ability and integrity as adult learners. This technique can be implemented at a later time in the class when a degree of trust (and feeling of safety) has been established. Admittedly peer review will not work well in every situation. However, looking carefully at classmates' work is a responsibility that adults will take seriously because they realize the importance of the task, want to be fair to others, and want to be treated fairly themselves. Part of the risk involved here has to do with the nature of the assignment. If high-stakes or graded writing in your course involves personal essays or other forms of writing where students might expose intimate aspects of their lives, this probably is not the place for peer review. But again, as we state in the chapter on assessment, asking learners how they would like to manage the assessment of their writing is good adult education practice.

Feedback on writing is where most of the learning will take place. It is important to be supportive and "kindly critical." Motivation for improvement will be influenced by the balance of encouragement and criticism. Too heavy a dose of negative feedback will be discouraging and may cause the learner to quit trying. It is important to give students hope and encouragement that they can improve.

The type of comments made on a paper also makes a difference. Simply noting errors is not helpful if the student does not know how to correct the errors. "Kindly critical" comments point the student in a specific direction for improvement. Also, unless your course is only about the mechanics of writing, be careful not to provide too much feedback on the grammar, spelling, and other aspects of the writing itself in the absence of remarks about the content of the paper.

Here are two examples of feedback comments that might be helpful:

> I like your ideas very much, but they are not always presented in a logical way. In your next draft, could you begin by writing an outline? This should help you organize your thoughts.

> You state your position strongly, but you are not comprehensive in covering other positions. I would recommend spending a little time with one or two of your classmates who have a different point of view and listen to their ideas. This will help you to widen your perspective.

A Few More Ideas

While there are many excellent books in the market that are intended to help people to develop writing skills, we have three favorites. One, *If You Want to Write* by Brenda Ueland, was written in the 1930s and was called by no less a writer than Carl Sandburg one of the best books on writing he had ever read. Fortunately it remains in print. The second book is a more modern version on a similar theme. *If You Can Talk You Can Write* by Joel Salzman is chock full of useful tidbits about writing. We know educators who swear by this book as a wonderful guide to help people who are afraid to write. And finally, *The Right to Write* by Julia Cameron (who is also author of *The Artist's Way* and other good texts about self-expression) was first published in 1998. It is easy to read and contemporary in its exercises and examples.

These three small volumes (small in size, but not in their power) are replete with encouraging thoughts and practical advice about writing. We end this chapter by selecting several of our favorite ideas from these three teachers of writing and sharing them with you. We hope something here may be inspiring or otherwise of help to you as you consider your own writing practice and also face the possibility of working as a teacher with your students' writing.

- *Let go of perfectionism.* Oftentimes we experience "writer's block"—not being able to get any words onto paper—because we feel that what we write has to be publishable or otherwise error-free. In the privacy of our own homes we can allow ourselves to deliberately engage "bad writing." Cameron suggests going to the supermarket and buying one or two tabloid newspapers. Read how badly some of those stories are written. And then sit down and write a tabloid piece yourself! The point here is to write. Get the hand moving on paper (or fingers on a keyboard). And don't fret about doing it "right," at least at first.

- *Write mindfully, heartfully.* Writing can allow us to slow down and see in more depth and detail the world in which we are living. Focus on whatever it is that captures your interest at a moment in time. This is what the Buddhists call living "mindfully." Another way of talking about it that may sound less cerebral is "heartfully." And it is interesting that buried within the word "heart" are both the word "art" and "ear." Writing, as Julia Cameron notes, is the art of the listening heart.

- *Be human.* Sometimes it is fear of not believing we have anything new or important to say that keeps us from writing. "I'm not original enough," is a complaint we frequently hear from students. And we like to respond: "Don't worry about being original. There's not much brand new out there in print. Worry about being human!" And what this means is that human beings are naturally curious—so write about those things you are most curious about. What are you interested in? Passionate about? Enjoy doing? Who or what do you love? These are the best topics to write about and they will also help you to listen to and become more familiar with some of the deepest chords of your humanity.

- *Be slow and patient.* What a counter-cultural thing to say to we Americans who seem to live so quickly! Fast food, drive-through banking, microwave ovens, rush hour traffic (which ironically forces us to slow down), speed pass cards . . . "Hurry up! Let's go! Keep moving!" But, as Brenda Ueland so beautifully states, the imagination needs "moodling"—long, inefficient, idling, dawdling time. "People who are always briskly doing something and who are as busy as waltzing mice have little, sharp, staccato ideas . . . But they have no slow, big ideas." So when you write, if large and juicy ideas do not come rushing into your mind right away, wait for them. Be patient. Go ahead and write down the little ideas so you'll have them to use later on to paint details around the larger and bigger idea when it finally arrives. The best writing requires percolation. This is one case—and we suspect there are many others—in our fiercely busy and rushed existence when slowness and patience pays wonderful dividends.

- *Criticism kills; praise nurtures*. The way to kill the spirit of creativity and desire to write is to strike it with blows of criticism. Ueland writes about the "teasing, jeering, rules, prissy teachers, critics, and all those unloving people who forget that the letter killeth and the spirit giveth life." We as teachers of adults are in an especially influential place vis-à-vis our students' writing. Take great care not to be overly severe. No matter what bravado some individuals may display in class, it has been our experience that most adults are highly sensitive and feel particularly vulnerable about their writing. If we paint their papers with too much "red ink," re-write every other sentence, and otherwise come down hard with the hammer of editing/criticism, there is a good chance our student will lose faith and not want to risk writing again. And this would be tragic because we as teachers have no right to deaden our student's spirit or in any way pose a barrier to their "right to write." It is our obligation as teachers to encourage learning and growth. A little praise can go a long way and inspire the desire to write more often (which usually eventually translates into writing better). It is true that sometimes we have to search hard to find things in our students' writing that are genuinely worthy of praise (giving false or groundless praise does nobody any good). But those gems—perhaps a metaphor, a particular word, or the way one sentence is so boldly stated—will be there if we look for them. Part of the art of good teaching is to seek and find such gems.

- **Writing is spiritual practice.** When we live in the present, which writing helps us to do, we are living spiritually. When we explore the depths of both our memory and imagination, which writing helps us to do, we are living spiritually. When we engage mind and the heart, which writing helps us to do, we are living spiritually. Teaching itself, as we hope we have been communicating all along in this book, is at its core a spiritual act. And teaching through writing further facilitates the act and enriches its consequences.

Exhibit 11-1

One-Page Sample from a Student Journal
Summary with Teacher's Comments

Of the programs we have discussed in class thus far that made up 19th century education, I have found myself mostly writing in my journals about Chautauqua. I have been fascinated by how this program, that started in Western New York as a Sunday School Teacher's summer camp with 200 people, grew in almost no time to involve millions across the entire United States.

What is the basis of your "fascination?"

One of my journals filled two entire pages on the idea of "Tent Chautauquas." When we talked about this in class I had a flashback to my grandmother telling me once that she used to go to tent shows as a young girl down in western Massachusetts. There would be storytellers, singers, and dancers. The kinds of things you would usually have to go into a big city like Boston to see. Grandma told me that it used to cost 25 cents and her mom and dad could afford to take all four of the kids. They would look forward to the tent shows coming to town every summer because this was not the kind of entertainment they had every day in South Hadley.

I love these intergenerational connections

I was also fascinated with the reading that said Chautauqua eventually developed into a full-blown college. Imagine that—"distance education" that we think is such a modern idea was actually taking place more than 100 years ago! In my journals . . .

Although, because of the times, this was exclusively a "correspondence school."

Exhibit 11-2

Math Autobiography

Name:_____ Date: _____

How do you feel about your prior math experiences? _____

_____

_____

_____

What have been your experiences with math teachers? _____

_____

_____

_____

Is there a time when you liked math? Hated it? Why do you feel the way you do?_____

_____

_____

_____

Do you have any special strategies for getting through math class? _____

_____

_____

_____

My Plan for Math Success

What do you want to accomplish in this class? List the math success goals you wish to achieve. Please be clear.

_____

_____

_____

_____

_____

_____

I want to achieve the goals because...

_____

_____

_____

_____

_____

These are the barriers or obstacles I may face and the steps I will take to overcome them.

Barriers   Steps to Overcome Barriers

_____   _____

_____   _____

_____   _____

_____   _____

_____   _____

These are the positive forces (help) I can use to achieve my math goal(s).

My Action Steps

_____

_____

_____

_____

The following people can help me in achieving my goal(s).

Name   Type of Help

_____   _____

_____   _____

_____   _____

Lastly, here are the steps I need to do in order to meet my math goals.

1. _____

2. _____

3. _____

4. _____

5. _____

6. _____

7. _____

8. _____

9. _____

Let's work together to accomplish these goals. I'm looking forward to working with you. Remember, my goal is to make you realize "Math Can Be Fun!"

Chapter 12:
Peer Learning

One observation we have made from many years of teaching is how much adults learn—and for the most part enjoy learning—from their classmates. In fact there have been numerous times when we have read in final course evaluations, "The best part of this course was learning from my peers!" While such feedback may not be the best food for our teacher's ego, we have learned to listen to the message it sends.

Peer learning has been talked and written about over the years under a wide range of titles: cooperative learning, collaborative learning, team learning, study groups, study circles, and work groups to name only some. While there are specific distinctions among each of these forms of peer learning, they have one common core: each involves learning activities in which students work closely with one another.

Many educators believe that we are moving from a dominant culture of competitiveness in schools to one of cooperation. This cultural seachange is also occurring in business organizations and other places of work. Just before he died, the well-known international businessman and consultant, W. Edwards Deming, wrote this: "We have grown up in a climate of competition between people, teams, departments, pupils, schools. We have been taught by economists that competition will solve our problems. Actually, competition, we see now, is destructive. It would be better if everyone would work together as a system, with the aim of everybody to win. What we need is cooperation."

Peer learning takes place by way of three basic types of group work.

Informal Group These are *ad hoc* temporary groups of students within a single class session. Informal groups can be as small as two people (often called "dyads") or as large as six or seven people. Their purpose is to discuss a question, solve a problem, or engage an exploration of an issue as part of an overall lecture or class discussion. Informal groups provide a change of pace and also give learners an opportunity to talk in a small group (which many people find easier than talking within the larger class). They can help to foster comfort and cohesion because students have a chance to get to know the people in their small group better than members of the larger class. Informal groups are the most common use of peer learning in the world of adult education.

Formal Groups These are teams that are usually established to complete a specific task. Examples of tasks might be to solve a math or science problem, prepare a position on a controversial issue, or perform a lab experiment. The duration of the formal group may be one or several classes. Typically, students work together until their assigned task has been completed.

Study Teams These are long-term groups, existing over the course of much or even all of an academic semester. The purpose of the longer commitment to a group is to provide learners with support, encouragement, and assistance. The larger the class size and more complex the subject matter, the more valuable study teams can be. Although they have been known to yield excellent results in selected situations (e.g., learning highly challenging and complex material, developing long-term group projects, or in courses where historically the dropout rate is high and people require a lot of support), study teams are not used as frequently as informal or formal groups in most adult education environments.

Several principles apply to using peer learning techniques effectively. First, it is important that the group feels the work they are undertaking is relevant. People must see the link between what you are asking them to do with group work and the overall goals of the course. Otherwise, it will be perceived as "busy work" and may be resisted. Second, it is helpful if interdependence among group members is designed into the task. The group needs to feel that it will "sink or swim" together, that each member is responsible to and dependent on all the others, and that one person cannot succeed unless all the other members of the group succeed. In other words, the activity should be designed such that multiple talents and voices are required to get the work done. Another principle is to introduce the opportunity for a fair division of labor. A larger project developed over an extended period of time works best for exercising this principle. An example from a U.S. history class would be to have various groups prepare a "Colonial America Newspaper" (this would fall under the category of "Formal

Group" as denoted above). Students would research various aspects of Colonial life and each member of a peer group would contribute one major article to the paper. Students conduct their research independently and use time in the group meetings to share information, edit each other's work, and design the layout of the newspaper. Building a degree of individual accountability into the cooperative experience is often necessary for peer learning to be effective (this diminishes the likelihood that one or two people will carry most of the work load).

Even within informal/short-term groups, individual roles and accountability may be designed into an activity. For example, we often use groups of four people to work on exploring a set of questions or solving problems. The groups themselves may be chosen randomly or by some other means. However, a note of caution: If you are aware of unhealthy dynamics between two or more individuals in your class, we suggest that you be directly involved with the selection of small groups and keep these individuals separated. Once the groups have been selected, we give the following set of instructions to one member of each group (this saves paper and also encourages a degree of interdependency, although it is also acceptable to give every member of the class a copy of the instructions).

Instructions for Group Problem-Solving Activity

Each member of the group will be an active participant and share her/his ideas openly. In addition to being a discussant, each member will also assume other responsibilities:

1. **Reader and Time Keeper**—*You have two jobs. You will read out loud to the group each of the problems you have been assigned to discuss and solve. You also must keep track of how much time you are spending on each problem so your group will be sure to deal with all the problems within the allotted time.*

2. **Checker**—*Your job is to keep the group on task. If you see the discussion moving off course, bring it back to the task at hand.*

3. **Reporter #1**—*Your job is to summarize the main points of the solutions your group comes up with and report them to the full class.*

4. ***Reporter #2**—Your job is to listen carefully to what Reporter #1 says during the debriefing and fill in any important ideas or details that she or he did not report.*

Common Complaints About Peer Learning

The practice of having students work together in groups, although praised by researchers, educational practitioners, and the vast majority of students, is not universally acclaimed. Here are some of the comments you may hear from students if you should decide to become a regular user of peer learning techniques:

"I paid my course fee with the expectation of learning from the teacher, not my classmates." Let people know from the beginning (and include language in the syllabus) that part of your course involves peer learning. Students who are adamantly against this practice may choose to drop the course. You may even want to build a small group activity into the first class to whet people's appetites for this kind of teaching-learning. There have even been occasions when people who thought they disliked student group activities came around to enjoy and benefit from them in a well-planned and facilitated adult education environment.

"Our group is not working together very well." In most cases it is important to encourage students to stick with it. Bailing out from a group is a last resort. You may have to invest more time with dysfunctional groups coaching members how to work effectively with one another to achieve the group's goals. Sometimes the learning that results from poorly working groups, exceeds that of highly functioning ones because students also learn important lessons in group dynamics and overcoming barriers. However, there may be occasions when the dysfunction of the group is so great that it is only leading people to feel a sense of failure and even despair. If such a situation presents itself and, after you have tried and failed with remedial interventions, it may be best to re-distribute members of the group. Of course, this action will have a ripple effect because other groups in the class will have to absorb a new member and that will change the dynamics of those groups. However, there are times when such re-arrangements may be necessary.

"I can get more done working on my own." While on the surface this may appear to be true, at least among some individuals, in the end it probably is not so. And quantity of work should not be confused with quality. Having three or four people involved with solving a problem or exploring an issue greatly enhances the capacity for critical thinking. Different students will bring different perspectives and assumptions to group work. Having even a minor disagreement about an idea or potential solution to a problem challenges students to examine their own perspectives/assumptions and perhaps change them. In job training-related courses this experience in teamwork is invaluable.

"We would accomplish more if the teacher lectures or otherwise presents this material to us." Again—maybe so. But is "more" always better? Active learning will yield deeper and longer lasting results than passively listening to the teacher's words. Peer learning activities are often, in fact, a wonderful complement (rather than supplement) to a lecture or presentation. It is true that lectures are an efficient way to communicate information. Group work is messier, more complex, and time-consuming. But peer learning through groups allows students to deeply engage ideas and often yields a richer overall learning experience.

"My group is O.K., but I'd much rather be with my close friends." Many people feel this way about their peer learning groups at first. Familiar people make us comfortable. But a random selection of students that results in a heterogeneous mix rather than letting people cluster into groups of friends often brings about a richer learning environment. Again, there is a greater chance that our thinking will be challenged by someone who is different from us. Consequently, the probability for deep learning (what one adult education theory calls "perspective transformation") is higher if our current thinking is challenged and we are forced to examine carefully what may be long-held assumptions. If there is resistance, you can always reassure your students that they can be with their close friends during the larger class sessions and during breaks.

There are a number of steps you, the teacher, can take to promote the success of peer learning activities in your course of study. First, be sure to allow sufficient time for the groups to develop into effective learning cohorts. We are not the most patient society, and expecting wonderful results from the first or second session may be unrealistic. Second, be specific about what you expect the groups to accomplish. Vague directions and/or goals will frequently yield only vague results. Third, invest an ample portion of class time for the peer groups to meet. While it is certainly acceptable, at least in some educational circles, to expect peer learning groups to meet outside of class time in order to accomplish their tasks, committing some class time signals to your students that this is indeed important work. Finally, be sure that you are available to meet with groups if they request it. During class time we find it useful to visit peer group sessions to gain a perspective on how the process is unfolding and what is being accomplished. If the groups are meeting outside of class time, your students may need to consult with you by telephone or e-mail. Your encouragement and, in some cases, technical support will go a long way toward ensuring that the peer learning experience is successful.

In sum, this brief chapter is intended to get you—the new teacher of adults—to consider the efficacy of using peer learning activities in your class. Considerable research has demonstrated that peer learning activities produce higher achievement, more positive relationships between students, and an overall healthier learning environment due to the cooperative nature of this work.

Chapter 13:
Instructional Media and Technology

This chapter will briefly describe a wide range of instructional media and technology "tools" that can help make you a more effective and efficient teacher of adults. Some of these tools have been around since your grandparents were in school. Others, particularly those that involve computers and electronic media, are more recent.

Our overall philosophy about instructional media and technology is that it ought to be used as a *supplement* and a *complement* to your teaching and not become the core of the teaching itself. We have participated in too many courses or professional workshops where the PowerPoint presentation itself dominated the dynamics of instruction, when the overhead transparencies more or less took over the class, or when flip charts in effect became the teacher. In our view this is not good adult education. On the other hand, a judicious and discerning use of technology that supplements and complements the efforts of a caring and thoughtful instructor makes your effort even more effective. Remember that adults prefer to experience a variety of approaches to learning.

Black/White Boards

Because a black or white board mounts the walls of almost every classroom in America, becoming in effect the "wall paper" of the school, most teachers take them for granted. This is unfortunate because this simple technology can be a teacher's best friend. Here are a list of "tips" about using black/white boards that we have picked up from our years of teaching:

- *Use the board to highlight the organization of your presentation and to emphasize your main points.* Writing an outline of the major points to be covered in a class is often a good way to start a session. Also, if you are lecturing, listing the key points of the forthcoming lecture is a helpful advance-organizer.
- *Have a plan for your black/white board writing.* Many adult students will copy into their notebooks whatever appears on the board. So you

want to be careful not to just write haphazardly because it might create chaos and confusion. Thoughtful and focused board work helps everyone to feel more organized.

- **When working with a white board, choose dark colors**. Black, red, dark brown, dark blue, green usually work well. But lighter colors—yellow, tan, pink—often do not. Between poor eyesight (among some adults) and glare from overhead classroom lights, white boards may sometimes be hard to read when writing with lighter colors.
- **Be selective**. Do not use the board to write everything! The idea here is to write out or illustrate the big ideas. Again, the age old princple "less is more" certainly applies to board work.
- **Write legibly**. This is an especially difficult challenge for some of us! We find that printing—as compared with writing script—helps. Also using BIG letters helps to ensure that everyone in the class can see these key ideas.
- **Read aloud while you are writing**. This technique allows students to write while you do. It is also serves as a reinforcement device. Additionally, there will be a number of students in your class who are auditory learners so reading aloud appeals to and supports their dominant learning style.
- **Be careful not to focus all of your attention on the board**. This is often a problem with almost any kind of instructional medium. The focus is on the medium (board, flip chart, screen) and the teacher forgets to make eye contact with students. This inattention to face-to-face communication can eventually become deadly and devolve the teaching into a mere listing of facts and ideas absent of meaningful human interaction.
- **Ask your students if they can see and understand the writing**. In other words, constantly "check in." It does no one any good if what you are writing seems incoherent, or cannot be read clearly, or otherwise is not helping people to learn.
- **Erase the board completely**. This is an important courtesy to the teacher who will be coming into your classroom tomorrow morning. Also—at any time during a presentation when you may be changing the topic— erasing the old work completely signifies that to the learner that "we are now on to a new subject."

Flip Charts

A flip chart is a large pad of newsprint (of varying sizes, but often 30" x 40") that rests on an easel or display stand. Flip charts can be used to display a series of prepared sheets or for spontaneous jottings. Here are a few guidelines:

- *Like a black/white board, flips are useful to highlight the organization of your presentation, to emphasize main points, and to stimulate students' interest.* They are particularly helpful for providing an outline of class, writing out difficult names or terms, showing diagrams or graphs, and summarizing major points. The flip chart is better than a black/white board from the perspective that much of this writing can be prepared in advance of the class or workshop.
- *Do not use flips when working with a large group.* If the room is large and people are seated more than 15 or 20 feet away from the pad, it will be very hard to see the words. While flips may be very useful, if at some point in the class a large group is broken up into smaller work groups (with each sub-group having its own flip chart and easel with which to work), it is generally not wise to use flip charts with a large number of people.
- *Use color.* This is another distinct advantage over black/white boards. Magic markers come in many shades and hues (and some even come smelling of different "flavors!"). Color can make a visual presentation more appealing and even work to help maintain interest among learners.
- *Make a record.* One of the things we like best about flip charts is that we can fold them up, take them home, and record important data that is stored on them for future use (e.g., typing them up as a reinforcing handout the next class; using the data on the flips for future reference in some other course or the next time we teach this course). This ability to record is particularly helpful when the class itself has made a substantial contribution to the material that is recorded on the flips. The teacher is saying something very important by the act of recording and later sharing these notes: "These ideas that you generated are important enough for me to record. I take them that seriously."
- *Use with small groups.* We like to use flip charts in small group work. Students write responses to a question or problem they are working on

and then bring the completed flip chart page(s) back to the full group for an at-large debriefing.

Overhead Projector/Transparencies

The overhead projector is a time-tested tool in teaching. It offers a degree of both flexibility and permanence that black/white boards and flip charts do not. For example, if created with a permanent marker, a good transparency may be used again and again. If created with a water soluble marker, a transparency can be erased in whole or in part and reused. Like both a board and flip, a transparency may be used to record student ideas. But unlike the other two, these records can be easily taken home to type for the class or otherwise share, and to store for longer term use. We know experienced teachers who have entire file folders of overhead transparencies—one for each course they teach. They are small, light, and easy to work with. Here are some concrete tips for their use:

- *Feel free to employ transparencies for many of the same purposes that you would use a black/white board or flip chart.* These purposes may include outlining the agenda for a class, introducing and/or reinforcing key points in a lecture, spelling difficult names or terms, and listing responses that come from students.

- *Make sure the words and images you have on the transparency are easily readable from the back of the room.* We like to arrive a little early on the nights we know we'll be using transparencies and set the overhead projector at an ideal distance from the screen. Then we take one or two of the transparencies we'll be using later in the class and do a "pilot test," focusing the lens if necessary, and walking to the back of the room to see if words and/or pictures can be seen without straining. If you are word processing a document that you wish to turn into a transparency, we recommend using 20 point font or larger. "Regular size" font—10, 11, or 12 point—is very difficult to read even from the front row of a classroom.

- *Less is more*. We have made and shall continue to make this point throughout this book. Sometimes the worst transparencies are the ones that overload the screen with information. Students feel overwhelmed by data overload. Small pieces of important material in bite-size chunks is the best way to both present and display information.

- **Turn off the projector when not in use.** Two problems occur when an overhead transparency is showing on the screen but the teacher is on to something else. First, this becomes a severe visual distraction. Some students will be back with the transparency instead of focusing on you and the new material. Secondly, projectors have built-in fans to keep the light bulb cooled during use. If the projector is running but without purpose, a noise distraction has also been created. This may become an especially difficult barrier for older students who may have difficulty hearing in the first place.

- **A brief delay.** It is good practice to wait a moment or two after you have projected a transparency onto the screen before speaking. This gives your students time to scan the material and get a feel for it as a whole. Leave the transparency up on the screen long enough for students to copy the material, but also let them know if you are going to distribute a handout that duplicates the image (even with a handout forthcoming, some students will prefer to still take notes because this is their preferred learning style).

- **When projecting a list, reveal only one item at a time.** A blank piece of paper may be used to cover everything on your transparency except the first point to be discussed. This line-by-line display both focuses learners' attention and helps to avoid sudden overload or the feeling of chaos with everything coming at once.

- **Use transparencies judiciously and in concert with other technologies.** This is our advice for you not to become like the little boy, called "Johnny One Note" by all his friends, who sang all day long but only sang the same note! We have all known teachers who have a preferred tool and go back to that tool again and again until it becomes highly predictable and perhaps even boring. While overhead transparencies are an effective tool, please do not rely on it too heavily (the same can be said for flip charts, PowerPoint presentations, or any teaching technology).

Videos

One of the best technologies in a teacher's tool box is the well-selected film or video. Films can help to create an experience and elicit emotion in ways that most teaching tools cannot. Sometimes the most memorable part of an adult education course is an artfully produced and performed film that has been judiciously selected as part of the curriculum. But maximizing the educational value from having your students view a film is not always easy.

- *Prepare learners for viewing the film.* Explain why you are showing this particular video and what you expect people to derive from it. Why is this film being shown in this course at this time? Does the film introduce new concepts, review material already covered, or pose a new problem? Preparing an advance-organizer with a small list of things to look out for in the story is often a good idea (but do not overload the learner with things to watch for—this will diminish both the learning and enjoyment).

- *Always preview.* One mistake busy teachers sometimes will make is to show a film only on the recommendation of a friend or colleague. This is your class and your responsibility. Taking 30 minutes, an hour, or substantially longer (which will be required in order to see a typical "feature film" in its entirety) is a major investment. You must be confident that this is a worthy investment *vis-à-vis* the goals of the course or workshop. In the case where the movie you wish to show is rated "R" or may otherwise raise issues of propriety, you may want to check to see whether or not your program has policies governing such films. This matter can become more complicated in a mixed-age environment where there may be concerns about age-appropriate materials.

- *Be present during the viewing.* You can learn a lot by observing your students during the film. Also, we have experienced that even when we are seeing a good film for a second or even third time there are new things to learn from it. You and your adult students are colleagues in learning and you do not want to create the impression that the film became an excuse for you to be out of the room doing something else.

- *Do not hesitate to interrupt the video at a critical point in order to exploit a learning opportunity.* One of the great things about a film in both VHS and digital virtual disk (DVD) format is that you can stop it at a salient point in order to talk about what has been going on. In some cases it makes good sense to "seize the moment" and work with an idea or situation in the story immediately after students have experienced it (as compared with waiting until the end). Keep in mind, however, that too many interruptions can be distracting, spoil the artistic experience of the film as a whole, and even dull the prospects of learning. Unless the video itself was produced with numerous "discussion breaks" built into the sequence (some educational films are), one or two well-timed stoppages should suffice.

- *Debrief*. After the viewing, it is important to engage the learner in some sort of debriefing exercise. You could facilitate a discussion, ask your students to write a "One Minute Paper," or have them break into small groups to talk about what they have just seen and learned. Sometimes timing becomes a problem, especially if you have shown a long film which has taken you to the end of the class period. In this case, asking people to debrief the film privately in some manner (e.g., write a journal entry about it, make a list of learning points, etc.) before the next class is a good practice. Then, in order to both honor the work the students have invested in their private debriefing and to harvest the learning that will derive from pooling individual responses, it is important to dedicate at least a modicum of time to a group debriefing at the beginning of the next class session.

Computer/TV-Assisted Lessons

This technology is used in many adult education districts. The teacher uses a television monitor or large white screen to show students images from a computer. Instead of attempting to walk around from person to person (seated at individual computer terminals) to bring everyone to the same screen, the teacher can focus everyone's attention toward the large projected image. The following five PowerPoint slides describe this technique in greater detail.

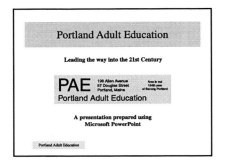

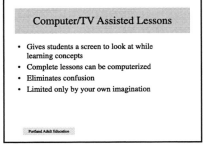

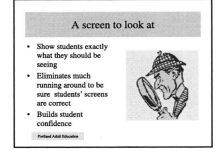

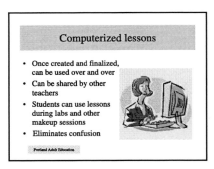

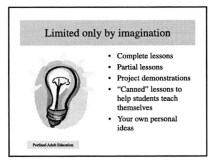

Computer-Based Presentations

A major trend today in teaching is the use of Microsoft PowerPoint and/or other computer-based presentation software. There are numerous advantages to using the computer to help you lecture or otherwise present course material. Your presentation will have a degree of pizzazz that hand-written flips or typed overhead transparencies do not. You can integrate visual images and color along with text. And you can store the data disk for future use, editing material as appropriate for another time and group of students.

It is important to point out that computer-based presentations are being used increasingly in a wide range of adult education courses these days—from insurance to reading to mathematics to social science. When used properly these can add great value to the teaching and learning experience. Before you make specific plans to use PowerPoint or other presentation software, however, please be sure to check with the adult education director to see what hardware and software resources are available for use in classes.

Having opened this section with such broad praise for the possibilities presented by computer-based presentations, why would an educational leader with the stature of Parker Palmer be quoted as saying: "I would like to see PowerPoint banned from education!"? In a recent visit to the University of Southern Maine we talked with Dr. Palmer about this matter. The reason he feels PowerPoint has been bad for education is that in many cases it reduces rather than increases student-to-teacher and student-to-student interaction. Everyone faces the screen (including, in many cases, the teacher) and directs attention at the slides of words and images. Teaching quickly devolves into another kind of entertainment. Or worse—there have been recent references made within educational circles to "PowerPoint induced sleep."

Of course, it does not have to be this way. It is also true that little or no attention to authentic human engagement during presentations could also occur with the heretofore mentioned technologies of black/white boards, flip charts, and overhead transparencies.

If you feel comfortable using computers in general and presentation software specifically, it is certainly worth giving this tool a try in your class. If you do, here are some guidelines you may wish to keep in mind.

- *Use fonts of 24-point or larger.* Font sizes smaller than this will in many cases be extremely difficult to read.
- *It is best to use dark type and a light background.* It is O.K. to vary this guideline on occasion, but try not to make a habit of employing lighter text.
- *Use the slide as a guide.* Do not read word for word. It is probably best, with the exception of an especially important or "juicy" quote, to only design key ideas and words as compared with long sentences into your presentation.
- *Don't get overly complex.* Microsoft PowerPoint and other software programs have numerous accents and capabilities that are designed to enhance the presentation. But over-use of text movement, sound effects, or other enhancements might distract from the goal you are trying to achieve. While a modicum of motion or other accent may at times be appropriate, we've heard from some adult learners how having sentences fly into view from the left or bottom of the screen slide after slide actually becomes annoying. "Keep it simple" is a good philosophy here and in many other situations in teaching (and in life).
- *Look into your students' eyes and engage them.* This is the point Parker Palmer was making. You don't want PowerPoint to make your students lazy or disengaged. And you don't want to focus all the attention—theirs and yours—onto the screen. There is a difference between teaching and entertaining. While good teachers also manage to entertain, this should not become the focal point of the activity.
- *Keep the room lights on (at least some of them).* It is not good practice to have a room darkened more than 15 minutes unless showing a feature film.
- *Make a copy of the presentation slides to hand out to students or otherwise make them available.* There is a print option that allows multiple slides to appear on a page and it is often good practice to print and hand out the presentation to students. If they have the slides during the presentation they can take notes on the handout. If for some reason you feel having all the slides in peoples' hands during the presentation will be distracting, you can tell people that a handout will be forthcoming

(some will choose to take notes anyway). Some teachers post their presentation slides on their personal Web pages or on "Blackboard" (another computer-based educational software) for their students to access. Several examples of PowerPoint print options are provided at the end of this chapter.

- *Have a back-up plan*. We have observed even the most experienced users of presentation software undergo difficulties with equipment and have to turn to "Plan B" on the spot. "Plan B" may involve having a set of overhead transparencies of the PowerPoint slides available. Or it may simply be that you end up working from the paper copies of the slides you have prepared for distribution. Things can and often do go wrong with computer-based presentations and it is best to plan for this contingency.

E-Mail

In 1990 almost no-one used electronic mail or—for that matter—had even heard of it. By the middle 1990s the use of e-mail was starting to become a regular communication tool in business and education, albeit not a universal one. Today nearly everybody has an e-mail account—with many having more than one—and use this communication technology on a daily basis.

E-mail can be a wonderful companion in teaching. Here is a brief list of ways we use electronic mail to work with our adult students.

- *Make announcements.* Creating a class distribution list enables you to send notices about upcoming events, reflections about some issue that may have come up in class, or other communications to students very easily. We have observed that, unless the use of e-mail is too frequent or about things that have little significance, students appreciate having these outside-of-class connections with their teacher.

- *Send advance-organizers*. Sometimes we simply forget to hand out an important advance-organizer to the class before some important work needs to be accomplished. And at other times we want to reinforce the importance of an advance-organizer by re-issuing it. E-mailing can help on both counts.

- *Share your reflections.* Often the best thinking occurs outside of school. We may have experienced a challenging learning unit or complex discussion in a recent adult education class that deserves more rumination. The facilitator sitting down to write a reflection about some issue that arose in class—after the dust has somewhat settled on that event—may enhance peoples' understanding. It also shows that you care enough about your work that you are taking time with it between class sessions.
- *Student-to-student communication.* We have written elsewhere in this book about the positive outcomes that often result from adult learners communicating directly with one another for feedback, support, and resource sharing. E-mail is an easy and efficient way of doing this. As their teacher you may ask members of your course to provide their e-mail addresses voluntarily early in the semester (the best time for collecting this information is usually during the first class). It is important that people understand this personal information will be shared with their classmates and that they agree to this. This directory, which may also include street/post office box mailing addresses and phone numbers, provides a valuable communication and community-building resource. E-mail, far more than mailing a traditional letter or talking by phone, is the preferred way of student-to-student communication these days.
- *Student-to-teacher communication* Some students feel intimidated expressing themselves or asking questions in class. However, they may feel safe posing questions or providing insights privately to their teacher through e-mail. Often, a teacher can use private e-mail correspondence as a springboard to encouraging more active participation in class.

Other Computer-Based Uses

As everyone knows, the world of computers is advancing rapidly and new applications of electronics to teaching and learning are constantly occurring. Since neither author has substantial personal experience with teaching via the Web, online conferencing using electronic discussion boards, or using computer-based course management systems, these technologies are beyond the scope of this book.

Our primary comment here is a cautionary one. We believe deeply that teaching is a human experience. And good teaching with adult learners involves authentic relationships between people. Even those people who teach computer courses (and we recognize there are a great many in adult education) and use the most advanced technologies available are engaged with their students. There are time-honored traditions to good teaching that represent sound practice regardless of the technology used.

We feel strongly that if e-mail communication and Web-based engagements can increase interaction between you and your students (they often can), and if they open opportunities for students' voices to be heard (they often do), these can be excellent facilitating tools. However, if instead of complementing and building capacity the use of computers only substitutes for teacher-to-student and student-to-student interaction, we stand against it. Like any other tool, the wonderful world of computer technology can be used for good or ill. Please be thoughtful and do not simply leap into the fray in order to feel that you are being "current" or "cool." There is simply too much at stake.

Sample of Power Point handout with six slides per page

Nurturing Voice and Spirit

- "I have something to say !"
- Builds confidence
- The meditative life
- Deeper self-understanding

- Three 20th Century movements have encouraged journal writing among the general population -
  - Growths of fields of psychology and psychotherapy
  - Women's movement
  - Personal spirituality

Three Research Questions

- What is the personal history of journal writing among older learners?
- What is their current journal writing practice?
- What benefits are derived from keeping a personal journal?

- "At a certain age you realize that living life is only the first step, then you've got to figure out what to make of your experiences, which is actually much more critical than the experiences themselves." (Patrick Delaney - protagonist in Jonathan Hull's novel, *Saving Julia*).

Sample

- 15 people (12 women, 3 men)
- 69.2 years (range = 57 - 81)
- 13 held college degree (8 of these also had a graduate degree)

Audience ?

- 10 people either have shared or plan to share their journals with family and/or close friends
- 3 were ambivalent about sharing journals
- 2 were determined not to share writing

Sample of Power Point handout with space for taking notes

Nurturing Voice and Spirit

- "I have something to say !"
- Builds confidence
- The meditative life
- Deeper self-understanding

_____
_____
_____
_____
_____
_____
_____
_____

Three Research Questions

- What is the personal history of journal writing among older learners?
- What is their current journal writing practice?
- What benefits are derived from keeping a personal journal?

_____
_____
_____
_____
_____
_____
_____
_____

Sample

- 15 people (12 women, 3 men)
- 69.2 years (range = 57 - 81)
- 13 held college degree (8 of these also had a graduate degree)

_____
_____
_____
_____
_____
_____
_____
_____

Chapter 14:
Teaching Online

Online education, that is learning via the computer without the benefit of a "live" or "face-to-face" classroom, will not be for everyone—teacher or student. But there is no question it is the fastest growing means of distance education today, far surpassing instructional television, compressed video, and other distance technologies that have been tried and faded in popularity. Like computers and the Internet on which it is based, online education is here to stay. In fact, every year adult learners are "voting with their feet" choosing computer-based learning over more traditional means because of convenience and access.

Quality of online teaching, however, has often been uneven and is a key area that requires attention if this fast-growing medium is ultimately going to serve well the needs and interests of adult learners. This chapter is designed to help guide the new teacher of adults who is working in an online environment to be a more effective instructor. In many ways the risk of having a less-than-stellar experience using computers is higher than with face-to-face instruction because of fear of technology on the part of many learners (and teachers!) and the potential depersonalizing influences of technology itself.

Before we get into the main content of this chapter, it is important to get a few definitions out of the way. First, let's talk about two terms that are used all the time in online education—asynchronous vs. synchronous. Asynchronous means "not at the same time." In other words, students will be logging into their computer course and contributing at different times of the day and days in the week. Synchronous means "at the same time" and there may be cases in which the expectation is for everybody is on their computers working together simultaneously. "Chat rooms" are usually synchronous, so people are more or less having a real-time conversation using written words instead of spoken ones. There are some online courses that use both asynchronous and synchronous experiences. Since our experiences teaching online have been of the asynchronous variety, and asynchronous learning seems to be preferred by the vast majority of online educational providers, it will be the primary focus of this chapter.

A second important term (and idea) to address is "platform." This is the actual software program that is used to conduct the computer course. Similar to the way physical classrooms in a school building will be different with regard to the number and location of white boards, whether there are desks or tables, the style of bookshelves, etc., online platforms will also vary. While there are a number of excellent (and continually improving) online platforms in today's marketplace, the one we are familiar with is called "Blackboard." You will therefore see graphic examples using this platform. By the way, choice of online education platform is not something individual instructors usually get involved with. These are decisions made by directors, school boards, and other administrators. Typically an orientation, online and/or in print, about the specific platform will be available to help you if you have had no previous experience with the platform. Online education platforms are increasingly user-friendly and designed for non-technical people (like Mike and Allen☺). Learning to navigate a platform can usually be accomplished, even by the novice, in a matter of a few hours. Additionally, most adult education programs have technical resource people to whom you can turn for assistance.

Now, let's get to the heart of the matter—ways to be effective as an online teacher of adults. In this chapter we shall discuss ten key factors that will contribute to you and your students having a high quality teaching experience online. Each of these factors will be explained using examples from our own recent online experiences. The ten factors are:

1.   Create and nurture a supportive learning environment
2.   Clear organization and communication
3.   Consistent teacher presence
4.   Cooperation among students
5.   Meaningful learning activities and assessment
6.   Prompt feedback
7.   Efficient course management
8.   Helping learners to stay on-task
9.   Accommodate learners' interests and learning styles
10. Support for technical problems

1. Create and Nurture a Supportive Learning Environment

Just like with face-to-face teaching, one of the first things that needs to be done with an online course is to create an environment where students feel safe, comfortable, and welcome. In many ways this is more difficult to do online because the teacher cannot smile warmly, use soft and non-threatening vocal tones, gesture, or some of the other ways we humans have to communicate friendliness. However, this essential foundation can be laid and good online teachers have learned specific ways to create such an environment.

One tried and true means of welcoming online students is to send them a letter in advance of the start of the course. Being able to do this will depend on the timing of course registration—it would be impossible to send a letter ahead of the start of your course if many students sign up only a day or two in advance. You will also need the support of your adult education program director. (E.g., printing the letter, gathering the mailing addresses, etc.) We strongly recommend that this initial welcome letter be sent via traditional ("snail") mail because part of what you will communicate are instructions about how to log onto the online platform, any password that might be required, etc. Keep the letter relatively brief (2-3 pages). Introduce yourself, say a little something about the goals of the course, how to obtain books and other materials, and whatever other information you deem important for people to have to begin your course. We also like to take the opportunity with this letter to share our enthusiasm for teaching and the fact that, although online education is still new to us, we are looking forward to learning with our adult students about both online education and the subject-at-hand. We have received feedback from a number of people that the fact that we even mentioned having feelings of discomfort or anxiety about online education in this letter helped them feel more relaxed and also got them to immediately sense that their instructor was indeed a co-learner with them in this new and challenging adventure.

Some online instructors will create an audio message that students can click on and listen to. This message can be combined with a PowerPoint presentation that reviews essential introductory information that is important to communicate during the start of any course. Advancing technologies make it easier each year to create such messages.

Just as you would do in a classroom, early in your online course (and most likely this will be your first "posting") there should be personal introductions. As the instructor, you can break the ice with your own statement, thus showing your students a model for content and style. If a friendly, open, and informal tone is created in this initial communication, the chances are good that these qualities will carry through to most or all other communications—and there will be many hundreds of them!—throughout the course. While we usually like to set a parameter of 50-75 words for a standard posting (this "rule" and others are established early in the course), an exception to this brevity can be made with these opening introductions. The more you learn about your students—and they about each other—the better. Exhibit 14-1 is an example of Mike's self-introduction in an online course entitled "Gerontology for Educators."

COURSES > HRD557 GERONTOLOGY FOR EDUCATORS (X6452... > COMMUNICATIONS > DISCUSSION BOARD > MESSAGE VIEW

Forum: Personal Introductions   Times Read: 29
Date: Fri Jan 13 2006 09:04
Author: Brady, Michael <e.brady@maine.edu>
Subject: Personal Introductions

I may as well get started with our HRD 557 introductions. I'll try to create a precedent in this personal introduction for both length and content. (Note— we'll talk about this early and often in our course, but ordinarily the best policy with regard to discussion board postings is "brief and cogent." Typically, this translates into 75-100 word statements that have been thought out beforehand. However, since getting to know at least some degree of detail about each other is an important aspect of creating an online community, let's not worry at this time about the length).

I am 56 years old and began my work in the field of gerontology as a young man :-). Actually, my first experiences working with older persons was as a community social worker in Connecticut in 1974. In the streamed video presentations that I have prepared for you (which we'll be viewing in early February) you'll hear several stories about those early days and experiences I had working with elders.

Professionally, as I believe I said in my letter, I have been in higher education much of my career and at USM since 1984. I actually have three jobs these days. I am a full-time professor (Adult Education, Gerontology, and a few other subject areas), I am a Senior Research Fellow at USM's Osher Lifelong Learning Institute (one day per week), and I am chairperson of the Department of Human Resource Development. These jobs keep me pretty busy and, on most days, happy.

Educationally I am a mongrel ("generalist" is what academic people usually like to say). I have degrees in Philosophy (B.A.), Religion (M.Div.), Social Work (M.S.W.), and Higher/Adult Education (Ph.D.). Suggested by this eclectic background is that I had a hard time sorting out my career goals. As part of my M.S.W. and Ph.D. programs I did quite a bit of work in aging, including two academic theses. Combining adult education with aging—a fancy term for this is "Educational Gerontology"—has been a core mission for me during the past nearly 30 years.

Personally I have been married 25 years and have three children. Our oldest, Ryan, is 24 years old and an intelligence specialist ("spook" is the term he uses) in the U.S. Navy currently stationed in England. Meghan just turned 22 and is a senior at McGill University majoring in political science and religion. Maura is a senior at Gorham High School and is looking at some very expensive colleges! (Anyone interested in granting us a low-interest loan?). My wife Nancy works at Unum-Provident in Portland. For hobbies I enjoy reading, writing (e.g., journals, memoirs, letters), riding my bicycle, taking long walks during all four seasons, and baseball. I am fortunate that my professional work allows me to marry vocation with avocation in a number of these interests, including baseball since I teach a summer course at USM about the game while traveling an average of 3000 miles by motor coach. "Baseball and American Society: A Journey," which has been taught once per summer since 1996, is my only undergraduate course.

One of the reasons why I remain interested in and passionate about teaching is that it provides me with ample opportunities to learn. I fact, I usually end up teaching subjects that I am interested in learning more about. I hope to learn a lot this semester from you and the literature and ideas we shall be exploring. I am looking forward to our online journey together.

Mike

Here are several other ideas you may wish to consider that will help you to create a welcoming and supportive learning environment:

- Create a "Coffee Break" forum where people can talk about anything, not just things related to the content of the course. Students can check in with each other about hobbies, their children, and other things that interest them. This will help to build a sense of community.

- Have a file in your course platform where people can post photographs of themselves.

- "Frequently Asked Questions" forum. This discussion forum, which can be made available throughout the entire duration of the course, is for posting questions about the syllabus, projects, assessment procedures, and/or other issues that relate to all students. You may use this forum to state questions that have arisen from your own experience or that have been asked by one of your students privately but clearly relate to everyone else in the course. An example of this might be: "What are the expectations for the number of postings we should strive for every week. The syllabus is not clear about this?" However, a FAQ forum is not the place for private or individual issues that inevitably arise in online teaching, such as "My computer went down last week and I'm feeling way behind in my work…"This kind of situation requires a one-on-one conversation, via e-mail or a telephone call, with the student.

2. Clear Organization and Communication

Good course organization is important in all teaching but may be even more so online. Adult students, especially those who are novices to distance education, will be anxious enough about this encounter. Having a poorly structured and chaotic electronic course site will only increase their nervousness and, worse, may cause their choosing to leave.

We have found that a solid syllabus, like with face-to-face instruction, is the foundation for sound organization. When teaching online, however, it often pays dividends to remind your students through announcements, course assignment postings, and/or frequent e-mail communications precisely what is expected of them on a week by week basis. (Or, as the case may be, two-week by two-week basis. In some situations, depending on the subject matter, two-week topical units work very effectively with online teaching.) In some ways it's safe to say that you can't be too repetitive with the communication of assignments and/or other important course activities. We're thinking of the famous mantra that military trainers often talk about: "Tell them what you're going to do; Do it; Then tell them what you did."

While some instructors who are technically proficient may wish to push the boundaries of whatever online teaching platform they are using, generally we suggest simplicity. Technological bells and whistles are not necessary for quality online teaching. Sound planning, provocative reading and discussion questions, and timely feedback is. The military has its mantra and so do we: Pedagogy (or, as it were in adult education, "Andragogy") always precedes technology. In other words, good teaching is good teaching whether it's using paper and pencil, a flip chart, white board, or an online platform.

A critical dimension of any good pedagogy/andragogy is clear and efficient communication. Times two with the posting of online messages. Just as students "listen" to thoughts as they are expressed aloud in a traditional class, everyone "listens" to ideas in online education by way of reading postings. Unless your instructions are otherwise (or small groups are being used where only individuals within an assigned group are communicating with one another in selected activities), everyone reads everything in an online course. So if you or your students use 250 words to communicate an idea that could have been well expressed in 50, everyone in the class is sacrificing efficiency. We usually like to create a "rule" early in the course that states, unless revoked in selected situations (for example with the initial personal introductions where you want people to say more, not less, about themselves), that all postings should be 50-75 words. We find that students honor this parameter and come to appreciate how, over the course of an entire semester, it saves a lot of time and enhances the experience. "Quality of communication, not quantity." Keep this general rule in mind for both yourself and your adult students.

3. Consistent Teacher Presence

Sometimes we learn a great deal from a bad experience. One year before he undertook his first online teaching experience Mike chose to participate in an online course as a student. He signed up for a course on the subject of "The History of Christianity" at a different university. The overall design of the course was to read books and discuss them using an online platform. (Note: this university did not use "Blackboard." But the platform itself was not the main problem.)

The readings were excellent. Students were asked to read about 100 pages per week and respond to a pre-set list of questions that were in the syllabus. So far, so good. But once the course began two things became immediately obvious. First, because the questions themselves asked students to define terms that were in the book rather than to give their viewpoint about the meaning of ideas or ways learners' believed these ideas in the history of Christianity influenced their lives, nearly every posting on the discussion board was the same. After the third or fourth lengthy definition of gnosticism or the Council of Nicaea (lengthy because there were no "groundrules" suggesting the number of words of each posting, and many students evidently believed that longer postings meant earning a better grade), weariness set in. After the 15th such posting Mike wanted to shut down his computer and take the rest of the week off.

The second concern about the course, which is the main point we are stressing in this section of the chapter, was that the instructor was mostly absent. Days went by, weeks went by, and students did not see a single posting on the board from him. Students responded to students (which was a course requirement, and a good idea), but seldom did the teacher have a presence on the board. Was he on vacation? Sick? Students had no clue. Once in a long while, like Punxsutawney Phil, the teacher would pop his head out of the ground (or into cyberspace, as it were) to check on our progress. But for all he contributed to our learning about the History of Christianity, he may as well stayed away. This experience, and ample research that has recently been conducted on this topic, suggests that consistent teacher presence is an important principle in effective online teaching. Otherwise, students may as well be taking a correspondence course.

While the frequency of teacher presence in a threaded online discussion will vary from course to course and forum to forum, depending on the specific nature of what is going on and the needs of the class, Exhibit 14-2 provides a "feel" for what we believe to be appropriate intervention. In this example from the spring 2006 version of "Gerontology for Educators" you can see that Mike introduces this discussion on March 2, contributes two postings in the midst of the conversation, and concludes the thread with a posting 16 days later. Note: All names except Mike's have been changed in order to protect the anonymity of the individuals who participated in this online course.

Exhibit 14-2

COURSES > HRD557 GERONTOLOGY FOR EDUCATORS (X6452 ... > COMMUNICATIONS > DISCUSSION BOARD > HOWARD MCCLUSKY'S CATEGORIES OF \"NEED\"

Link to Our Explorations?	Mike Brady	Thu Mar 02 2006 09:53
Re: Link to Our Explorations?	Carol Ann Schools	Mon Mar 06 2006 20:02
Re: Link to Our Explorations?	Larry Scizzi	Mon Mar 06 2006 21:39
Re: Link to Our Explorations?	Tom House	Thu Mar 07 2006 13:33
Re: Link to Our Explorations?	Erica Dorfman	Tue Mar 07 2006 13:57
Re: Link to Our Explorations?	Nicole Santana	Fri Mar 10 2006 09:26
Re: Link to Our Explorations?	Mike Brady	Fri Mar 10 2006 09:14
Re: Link to Our Exploratio...	Susan Johnson	Fri Mar 10 2006 09:51
Re: Transcendence	Bill Williams	Sat Mar 11 2006 12:38
Re: Link to Our Explorations?	Nicole Santana	Sat Mar 11 2006 09:32
Re: Link to Our Explorations?	Marijane Lowry	Sat Mar 11 2006 14:41
Re: Link to Our Explorations?	Elizabeth Ellsworth	Sat Mar 11 2006 12:54
Re: Link to Our Explorations?	Stephen Norland	Sun Mar 12 2006 20:53
Re: Link to Our Explorations?	Erica Dorfman	Mon Mar 13 2006 08:33
Re: Link to Our Exploratio...	Carol Ann Schools	Mon Mar 13 2006 11:53
Re: Link to Our Explora...	Larry Scizzi	Mon Mar 13 2006 21:18
Re: Link to Our Expl...	Mike Brady	Tue Mar 14 2006 18:45
Re: Link to Our Explorations?	Marijane Lowry	Thu Mar 16 2006 22:29
Re: Link to Our Explorations?	Mike Brady	Sat Mar 18 2006 09:13

4. Cooperation Among Students

The key ideas about the importance of creating opportunities for adult learners to work with each other are discussed in greater detail in Chapter 12 ("Peer Learning"). Once again, to prevent your online class from quickly degenerating into an electronic correspondence course, it is important to find ways for students to interact with one another. Have them work in small groups on a problem or question, assigning or having each group select their own "chairperson" to report the big ideas they discussed to the entire class. Have your students, as the otherwise mostly absent teacher in "The History of Christianity" course mentioned above did—and to his credit—respond to the ideas posted by classmates.

Sometimes immediately jumping into small groups can be confusing, since it often takes a week or two for learners to get their "sea legs" and begin to feel comfortable with the online platform, assignments, and other aspects of your course. We suggest that the initial group activity be done in pairs to facilitate students' ability to contact each other (either in the "Groups" section of the platform itself or via e-mail) and then grow the group size over time. One of the problems with larger groups is the different personal work schedules of members wherein some individuals may be doing most of their course work on weekends while others are working during the week. If there are assignments that require small groups to "meet" together and then report out their key findings, synchronizing schedules within each small group often presents a challenge. (By the way, this is one of the advantages of the two-week unit. It gives small groups more time to meet, discuss, and report out.)

Even though it is important for groups of students to be working together and learning from each other as peers, it is also important that the online teacher interact with each of the small groups on a consistent basis. Ask questions. Provide input. Nudge the small group toward its goal. Be present and supportive but not intrusive.

5. Meaningful Learning Activities and Assessment

Just like in face-to-face teaching, adults need engaging activities that are authentic and meaningful, ones that have a real connection to their lives. Exercises for the sake of exercises won't do. Just because a course is online does not mean that you can't have students practicing a hands-on activity, investigating a community problem, making field observations, or engaging some other application, synthesis, or problem-solving activity.

Similarly, assessments need to be meaningful. Please review what we have to say about assessing learning in Chapter 15. While giving an oral presentation may not be as easy to accomplish as in a traditional classroom, online students can nonetheless provide a videotaped presentation that can either be viewed privately or video-streamed and uploaded into the platform for everyone in the course to see. PowerPoint presentations can be created by students and shared. In fact, entire portfolios of learning can be presented electronically. If formal testing is in order, most of the online platforms have special areas within which these assessments can be organized. While indeed some projects and assessments are more difficult to perform via the computer than in person, it is nonetheless vitally important to try to make these learning activities as meaningful and authentic to the lives of your students as possible.

6. Provide Prompt Feedback

Providing feedback on student work is one of the most important tasks for distance teachers. Commenting on and correcting students' work not only provides the adult learner with relevant input, but allows you to build a relationship. Methods of providing feedback may vary depending upon the design of the course—for example, is it a 100% online experience or are there blends of online with several face-to-face meetings or teleconferencing? (By the way, our strong recommendation is not to "blend" technologies when teaching online, with the exception perhaps of a phone call once in a while to nudge someone along or to solve an individual problem. When people sign up for an online course they expect that they'll be able to work from their home or office computer and will not have to drive to a compressed video location or to a classroom somewhere to rendezvous with their teacher and classmates. Also, if you have students from outside the local geographical region it simply is not practical—or fair—to require them to travel in order to be a part of your course.)

In a recent report issued by the Institute for Social Research in Ann Arbor, Michigan entitled *Handbook of Distance Education for Adult Learners*, the authors enumerated a variety of strategies for maintaining frequent contact and providing effective feedback to students-at-a-distance:

- Send e-cards encouraging students and praising accomplishments

- Send individual, rather than group e-mails to learners, in order to make the feedback more personal

- Send e-mail messages which ask questions and prompt students to think about their learning goals

- Offer assistance to locate information on the Internet that could help learners to accomplish their goals

- Telephone students who had not been active for a period of time to encourage them to stay in the course or program

- For equity purposes, and also to develop a closer relationship with them, telephone those students who have remained vigilant and active in the online course and focus your conversation on their interests, concerns, and goals

- For those who may live within a reasonable commute, offer drop-in times for students who want assistance in person

- Consistently use praise and positive feedback on students' work

- When providing negative feedback, always be constructive and point toward specific ways students can build on strengths to improve performance

- Work with each student to help them see how the content of your course relates to situations in their lives and to their own personal and professional goals

One final comment is in order here. When providing feedback it is good to consider the "three day rule." No important statement posted on line (there are some postings that are more or less routine and do not always require instructor's response) and certainly no private e-mail sent by students to you should go more than three days without a response. Intervene while the issue-at-hand is still "hot." Waiting more than three days to respond may mean the student has moved along in her/his learning, sometimes quite a great distance, and the significance of your response will be greatly diminished. Waiting long to respond also communicates to the student that s/he is not that important to you in the greater scheme of things. That's not a message an online instructor —or any teacher—wants to communicate.

7. Efficient Course Management

We're going to keep this seventh principle, and the final three that follow it, brief and simple, "efficient" as it were. As you know, if you have had experience with online education, as a teacher or as a student, it can be very time consuming. In fact, both new and experienced online practitioners estimate that it takes twice the time to prepare and teach online as it does in a traditional classroom environment. Therefore it is extremely important that what you do is efficiently managed. Be clear. Be parsimonious. Don't waste everyone's time writing long diatribes or having your students navigate labyrinthine pathways on the computer. You will be more effective and will have more fun—and your students will both appreciate and benefit from—an orderly, efficient, and well-managed online classroom.

8. Helping Learners Stay on Task

Here is a brief list of ways that you, the online teacher, can help your students stay focused and "on task:"

• Schedule assignments with specific due dates

• Send reminders—as "announcements" in your online platform or through e-mails—about upcoming due dates

• Have a number of smaller projects scheduled over time rather than one large one due at the end of the term

• Encourage students to self-evaluate and share with you their progress on meeting goals at various points in the course. (This activity also encourages critical self-reflection and independent assessment).

• As another function of "checking-in" and critical self-reflection, invite your students to keep a learning journal in which they write about what they are finding most interesting, difficult, surprising, etc. (Depending on the nature of the course, the level of maturity and confidence of the learners, etc., these learning journals could be kept private and "for their eyes only" or shared, in whole or part, with you)

- Provide constant encouragement and continually remind students of the larger goals of the course and the progress they have been making toward accomplishing those goals

9. Accommodate Learners' Interests and Learning Styles

Here are some things to keep in mind with this important factor:

- It is usually safe to assume that your students have a basic interest in the subject matter that you are teaching by virtue of the fact that they have registered for your course. (The exception here is education or training that is mandated in order to get a license or certificate). You can check in with learners during the first few days of an online course about their specific motivation—Why are they here? What do they hope to learn? Having answers to these questions, and students having the opportunity to expressly name their interests and goals, will help set the stage for a healthy learning environment

- Create choices. Try not to have a single assignment but give options for accomplishing the important work in your course in a variety of ways.

- If possible, employ multiple methods of assessment. In most educational situations there are numerous ways to measure what people have learned. If adult learners have a choice about whether to write a paper, create a portfolio, or make a presentation, they are more likely to remain enthusiastic about their learning.

- Teach with diverse methods. While admittedly this is easier to do in a face-to-face course, it is nonetheless possible with online education. Technology is improving every year such that including video presentations, graphics, music, and other accents do not take a great deal of special talent or time. Mix small group with large group discussions. Have students go out into their communities to explore issues and report back to the class online. While admittedly a great deal of online teaching and learning involves writing and reading text, looking for alternatives to writing and reading on a computer monitor will help to ensure that students with different learning styles will have their needs met.

10. Support for Technical Problems

In some ways, unless you are highly computer savvy yourself, this factor is out of your hands. There will be people in your school's administration or technology center that will be available to assist students who are experiencing problems with their computers or the online platform you are using for your course. Your job is to (1) be aware of problems that your students are experiencing and (2) ensure they are able to receive assistance in an timely fashion. Placing a phone number for technical assistance in the syllabus is often helpful. Having a discussion forum specifically dedicated to issues with technology is often a good idea. (Learners will often help each other to solve problems if given such a forum). Periodically asking your students by way of posted announcements or special e-mail communications about how they are doing with the technological aspects of your course will also help you to be able to help them. In summary, the important thing here is to stay vigilant. One of the reasons students drop out of online courses is because they have a glitch with the technology, fall behind in their work—sometimes it only takes several days of missed work for people to feel they have fallen behind—and then, feeling pressure to catch-up or otherwise frustrated, they choose to leave the course. Knowing there is help available, and knowing that their teacher cares enough about them that s/he is willing to mediate matters related to technology, will enhance course retention and also help to ensure that adult students have a successful online learning experience.

In summary—during the three years between the first and second editions of *The New Teacher of Adults* we have seen online education explode across the adult and higher education landscape. The technology that supports distance education will continue to change (and we assume improve) rapidly. There is no telling what new platforms and "bells and whistles" will be available in the marketplace for those who wish to teach and learn online. However—and this has been the underlying principle throughout this chapter and in fact the entire book—we believe that good teaching is good teaching.

No matter what direction online education takes in the future, then as now pedagogy will always precede technology.

Chapter 15:
Three Simple Tools: Advance-Organizers, Mind Maps, and the "Minute Paper"

Advance-Organizers

An advance-organizer is a tool the facilitator uses to help students prepare for a specific unit of study. That unit may be as small as a 30-minute discussion or as large as the entire course itself. It is a "focusing" tool that, if employed skillfully, can save time in class and enable the adult student to enhance opportunities for learning.

The most common use of an advance-organizer (sometimes also called advance-planner) is to help people prepare for a single class assignment. Let's say, for example, that in your literature class you have assigned the famous novella by Leo Tolstoy, *The Death of Ivan Ilyich*. It may well be that it is in the best interest of the individual learners and the course as a whole to simply ask people to read the book and say to them "come to class next time prepared to discuss it." Afterall, *The Death of Ivan Ilyich* is not a long book, in some editions it is only 90 pages. Perhaps you are simply interested to learn what people got out of the novel or how they liked it. If that is the case, then "come to class prepared to discuss it" may work just fine (by the way, that statement in itself is an advance-organizer, albeit a soft and overly general one).

However, if you have more specific and layered reasons for having assigned this novel, it is best to help people think about these before they come to class for the discussion. Do you want your students to focus on specific characters in the story? Do you want them to be thinking about the style in which Tolstoy wrote his novel? Do you want your students to identify the emotions that accompany Ivan's encroaching death? Particularly if you are teaching this book as part of a social science course instead of a literature one—which is often the case with *The Death of Ivan Ilyich*—one of your chief goals may be to have people observe Ivan's family and other social support systems. How do his wife, daughter, friends, and professional colleagues interact with Ivan? Or is a key objective for reading this story to have your students explore and be able to explain the basis for Ivan's remarkable epiphany in the final scene?

Each of these lines of questioning will take the class on an entirely different learning journey. Without helping people to focus their attention in advance of the discussion, you take the risk that the dialogue around *The Death of Ivan Ilyich* will be overly broad and perhaps unclear. Even the most diligent student will not be sure about what to prepare in advance and will—at least in many cases—not have confidence going into the class discussion. We believe it is an important part of your job as a teacher to help guide the discussion toward meaningful results. And we also believe that nurturing the learner's confidence is a crucial aspect of effective teaching.

While advance-organizers are most commonly used to help a class prepare for group discussion, they may also be used in advance of a lecture. Are there specific pages or chapters in the text book that will help students tune—in more crisply to what you will be lecturing on during the next class? Are there questions you may ask them to think about (and perhaps write out responses to) that will help the learner to make connections with the ideas you will soon be presenting? These can be "hooks" for the adult learner on which to hang pieces of information.

Perhaps the simplest kind of advance-organizer is sharing with students an outline of upcoming topics. Some teachers will do this the week before to provide ample planning time. Other instructors will provide their class with exercises or detailed materials weeks in advance or even for the entire semester (these would specify "things we will be doing" that aren't necessarily outlined in the course syllabus). But even listing the topics to be covered that night on the blackboard or on an overhead transparency is useful to show your students in which direction they will be traveling during the next several hours. In recent years some teachers have used e-mail to communicate in advance the overall themes that will be treated during the next class (perhaps accompanying this message with a nudge to prepare in a certain way or a compliment about good work that was done during the last class).

As mentioned at the beginning of this section, in the case of intensive institutes or courses that are run over a brief period of time, advance-organizers take on a greater sense of urgency. Here is one example from our practice. For the past eight summers Mike has organized a travel-based course on the subject of baseball and American society. What makes this course unique (in fact, it is the only one of its kind in the United States) is that the teaching and learning take place on a 45-passenger motor coach. Students board the bus—usually on a Friday or Saturday morning in July—and travel to large cities (New York, Chicago, Philadelphia, Baltimore) and small ones (Oneonta, Pittsfield, Akron, Fort Wayne) to study baseball and its place in the American story. Several months before the bus departs, those who have registered are mailed a detailed advance-organizer. This document not only tells them, much like communications that are mailed to customers of a travel agency, what clothing and supplies to bring along on the trip, but also focuses peoples' preparation for the course of study. Assigned books are listed. A larger bibliography is included (this is important because one of the course requirements is for students to select one book of her/his choice from this large bibliography, read it, and prepare a report that will be shared with the rest of the class on the learning journey). And writing assignments are carefully spelled out.

When people arrive on the morning of departure much of their work is already done. They have read, thought about key issues the course is designed to cover, and have already drafted a fair portion of their writing. All of this has been accomplished even before stepping onto the bus! What this advance work does is puts everyone on a common footing because everyone has read core required books and written about some of the same questions). This, in turn, facilitates group bonding and the development of a learning community. Because we have done this work in advance, as we travel across America using the motor coach as a moving classroom (on the bus we have brief lectures, students present their oral book reports, we watch and discuss videos, and debrief our experiences in cities and ballparks) we are operating on a higher plain than we would without having advance preparation. We have, if you will, "jump started" the learning. People tell us again and again that the work done in preparation for the travel and other learning experiences in this baseball course are a crucial dimension in the total experience and greatly enrich it.

Another example of an advance-organizer comes from a job readiness section of a course that one of us teaches.

Please prepare in advance of our class on Jan. 27:

We will have a class discussion of methods of handling dis-agreements at work. How to handle criticism. How to resolve problems in the workplace. Please write about the following in your journal:

"Everybody has difficult moments at work. How do you handle a conflict with a fellow worker or supervisor when it aris-es? Please be specific."

In summary, we see a number of advantages and potential benefits with the use of advance-organizers in teaching:

- It serves as a kind of "map" to where the next unit of study is going
- It focuses the student's attention to the issues that are most important in the particular course of study
- It helps to make group discussions more efficient and effective
- It enables the learner to come into a discussion or lecture with greater confidence that she or he is "prepared"
- And because advance-organizers help to create a common ground of preparation, they can help to contribute to a greater feeling of community among the learners

Mind Maps

Before we talk about mind maps, we'll show one. What better way to explore the possibilities of using mind maps than to see one about the tool itself?

A mind map, sometimes also called a concept map or "web," is a way of displaying ideas graphically. It is a kind of "organized brainstorm." A mind map is a tool that can be used both publicly in class (e.g., creating a map on a chalk board or flip chart with the whole group) or privately by you and your students to gather ideas into patterns.

The process begins with a central idea, something important that relates in a core manner to the work you want to accomplish in class that day. Typically, this core idea is one you select based on your goals for that particular class. For example, in an introductory graduate course in adult education, early in the semester I work with my students to mind map the concept, "Adult." I write the word "Adult" in the middle of a large blackboard and draw a circle around it. Then I ask the group, "What ideas do you associate with this concept?" As students brainstorm correlates to "Adult," I write them on the board. Early in the process the mind map might look like this:

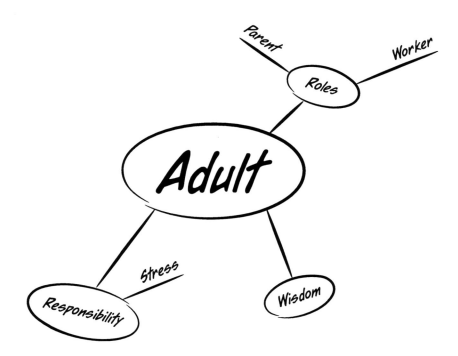

Students, at all stages of this process, have the option of making a link directly to the core concept of "Adult," or to one of the subsidiary ideas. I often ask, when students speak out their concept (I'm usually doing the writing, but you can call upon the assistance of one of the members of the group to record if you'd like), if they would like that particular contribution to the map linked directly to the core idea or to one of the correlated ones. So the mind map builds:

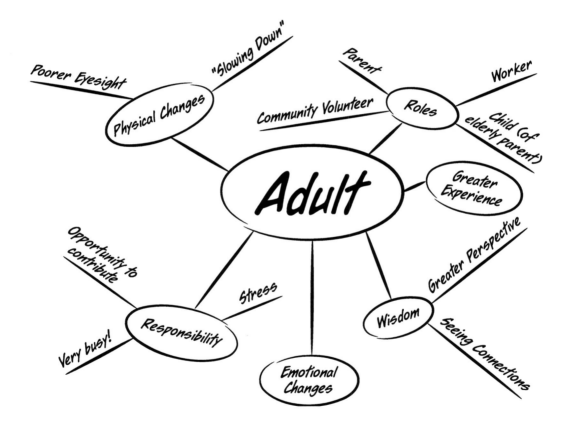

There is software available today that enables you to construct mind maps electronically. One of the most popular ones is called "Inspiration." If you have the interest and easy access to computers in your classroom, creating a mind map electronically might prove to be useful. But a simple in-class mind map is easily accomplished with a black/white board or flip chart (Caution: the problem with a flip chart is the limited size of the space available with each page of paper. It is important for everyone to be able to see the entire mind map at all times so they can choose where to build connections. Lots of pages and masking tape may be required to build your map with flips!).

We have also enjoyed productive experiences having students do their own mind mapping in class in small groups. If there are only three or four people working on a map, it is easy to have them do this on flip chart paper (the writing can be made small enough to fit numerous words/ideas on the page and still have people see everything). In this same history and philosophy class, after we do a large-group mind map of the concept of "Adult," I break up the class into small groups and have each group spend 15 minutes mind mapping the concept, "Adult Education." Then we come back together as an entire class and share our maps with each other. If used this way as a small group activity mind mapping can be an excellent team-building exercise (see Chapter 5 about creating class assignments).

We have learned over the years that some students like mind mapping as a way of preparing for important papers or projects. It is a more left-brain way of outlining or organizing ideas. In some cases we even allow students to submit their mind maps as part of formal assignments. Doing so allows the teacher to see something of the development of students' ideas. It is also an important way of honoring different learning styles and giving each adult learner space for her/his own creativity.

Exhibit 15-2 and 15-3 display two additional examples of mind maps.

The "Minute Paper"

This simple device, which is said to have been invented by a physics teacher in California, is potentially one of the most effective teaching tools we know of. Some time in the middle of a presentation or other curriculum unit, ask your students to take out a piece of paper and write for "a minute" (or three minutes, or five) about what they have learned thus far. Variations of this exercise might be to ask them to "list three big ideas," "state the most important questions" they have about the topic at hand, or "write about the best application of the ideas just presented to your own life or work."

Some teachers like to announce in advance that a "Minute Paper" will be written some time in the middle of the class. That is an advance-organizer of sorts and may pique students' attention. Other teachers like to simply stop the presentation or discussion at some appropriate point and conduct this summary exercise. Short time periods for writing usually work best because having people write for more than five minutes might begin to feel like a test. At times we'll simply ask students to write in their notebooks while at other times we have prepared a page of paper, that is mostly blank, and titled (e.g., "Five Minute Paper on the Causes of the Civil War") that we hand out for this exercise.

This "Minute Paper" can be used in numerous ways. In many cases the written response is for the eyes of the student only. It is therefore a didactic device that enables the learner to summarize her/his thoughts about main ideas in a particular subject and at a particular time. At other times the teacher wants to read these brief summaries in order to ascertain how clearly the lecture has come across. Are most people picking up the main ideas? Have I been making the main points clearly? So it can be an important feedback device.

Another excellent use of the "Minute Paper" is to debrief a film that has just been viewed or a guest speaker who has just visited your class. Wilbert McKeachie lists additional questions that may be asked as part of this brief in-class exercise:
- What do you think about this concept?
- Give an example of this concept or principle.

- Explain this concept in your own words.
- How does this idea relate to your own experience?
- What are some of your feelings as you listen to these ideas?
- How could you use this idea in your own life?

Finally, the flexibility of this teaching tool is enhanced by the fact that it can be used with a class as small as three or four students and one as large as several hundred. When working with a larger class, you may wish to ask students to debrief their "Minute Paper" in dyads or groups of three. This can be yet another way to get people to know and learn from one another.

Exhibit 15-1

Sample Advance-Organizer
(In this case handed out to the class one week in advance)

Please prepare responses to the following questions based on your reading of Leo Tolstoy's *The Death of Ivan Ilych*. There is no need to completely write out your answers to these questions because these papers will not be collected. However, during the next class we want to have a meaningful discussion of this book so it is important to have thought carefully about these issues.

1. What do you think of Ivan Ilyich as a person? Do you like him? Do you "respect" him? Why/why not?

2. What would you say are Ivan's greatest fears as he learns of his diagnosis? In what ways—if at all—do these fears change over time as he grows more ill?

3. Were you surprised by the ending of the book? Why/why not?

4. What major theme or message do you think Leo Tolstoy was trying to communicate in this story?

Exhibit 15-2
Mind Map for New Teacher of Adults

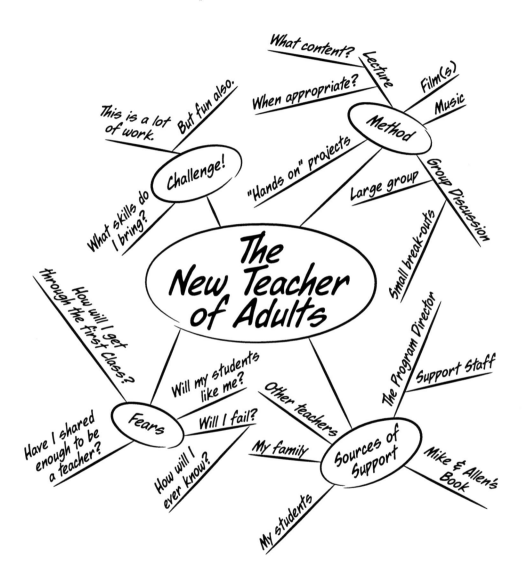

**Exhibit 15-3
Mind Map for Finding a Job**

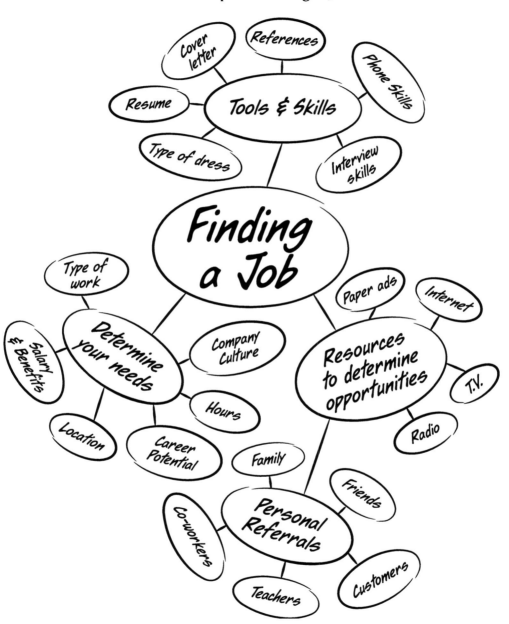

Chapter 16:
Co-Teaching: Working with Others in Your Classroom

Teaching is usually considered a solitary profession. Many of us spend the majority of our classroom time in relative isolation (excepting our students of course), with little or no interaction with other professionals or teachers. This does not always have to be the case. As you gain confidence in your teaching abilities and meet people and organizations related to your course content, you may want to invite people to come into your classroom to help. Obviously, this will be done on a class-by-class basis, clearly dependent on what you are teaching. For example, if you are teaching a course on how to buy a house, or real estate in general, you might consider having a real estate professional join one of your classes to help co-teach a particular section. Adult learners generally enjoy having their day-to-day (or night-to-night) classes broken-up with different teaching approaches. It makes the class more fun and provides learners with different perspectives. The purpose of this chapter is to provide three basic co-teaching models. Some may be applicable to your particular situation and others may not. The key is to identify what type model(s) may add texture and meaning to your students' (and your) classroom experience. Here are three co-teaching models to consider.

Former Student Model

One of the most effective ways to establish credibility with your students is to have a former student join your class. Let's stick with the real estate example mentioned above. You could invite a former student in who has successfully navigated the home ownership process from taking your class to buying a home. This would be a great opportunity for your former student to share their experiences with your current class. Using former students in this capacity has the potential to add real meaning for your adult learners. In addition, your class can ask questions of your former student about their experiences in the class and its direct applicability to home ownership. These types of classroom exchanges can be extremely useful to your students.

Furthermore, using former students can also be particularly effective working with 'at risk' learners. For example, if you are teaching a class that is related to job hunting/training (i.e. resumes, interviewing skills, networking, etc.) you may want to have a former student who has been successful in getting a job join your first class to talk about their experiences in finding work. At the risk of insulting some of our readers, adult education teachers may not always possess the same level of credibility that a former student may have. Your current students can draw direct, personal connections with a former student that is simply not possible with an adult education teacher. Having successful former students interact with your current students can provide demonstrable, concrete "success images" to your adult learners. Also, adult learners often feel more comfortable in asking former students questions. On several occasions we have seen our call for questions or comments go unanswered only to have, a half-hour later, a former student guest speaker bombarded with questions!

One word of caution—If you decide to invite a former student (or even a panel of former students) into your classroom, it is important to give them clear parameters of what you want them to talk about and what questions you will be asking. Encourage them to write out preliminary notes. Former students, like most of us, are not always comfortable with public speaking. The more structure you provide along with a sense of predictability will go a long way towards helping your former students feel more comfortable in coming back to your class.

Using former students can help you establish a safe learning environment. Obviously, using former students is not for every situation, but it can serve a useful purpose in your overall teaching strategies. Talk to other teachers and administrators about using this approach. They may have useful suggestions on how best to proceed with its use.

Corporate/Non Profit Partners Model

In certain situations, we have asked professionals (non-teachers) to join us in our classrooms. Depending on course content and what you are trying to accomplish, having individuals from the private/public sector join your class can add valuable insights and perspectives to your students' experiences. It really all depends on what you are teaching and its applicability to the students' learning experiences. The real estate professional scenario that introduced this chapter is a good example of how you might utilize this particular model.

Use of private sector professionals can also be extremely helpful when teaching job training courses. We regularly employ human resource professionals in our classroom curriculum when teaching job hunting, interviewing skills, or resume building. Students gain valuable insights and feedback from these encounters and begin to understand the importance of networking for potential job opportunities and how the course content is directly related to creating a career. Conversely, the professionals who join the class often talk about how much they also gain from the experience. You will be surprised on how open professionals are to the opportunity of joining your class. This is truly a win/win model for all concerned.

Additionally we have also used professionals to help in courses as diverse as Business English, Workplace Communication, and Customer Service. It really depends on the subject at hand and how you want your students to understand the content and its applicability to the world outside the classroom. We can easily see professionals used in enrichment classes such as gardening, home improvement/repair, music, art, cooking, and many, many more. It comes down to what you are trying to accomplish, the length of the course, and your district's guidelines.

The Full Co-teaching Model

On occasion, both authors have worked with other adult education teachers in a complete co-facilitation partnership. This can be an interesting and valuable experience. Of course, having two teachers for a single class may bump into budgetary barriers for the institution. However, even on a limited basis, this experience can add great value to your teaching. For example, Allen has had the opportunity to co-teach a workplace communication class with other adult educators for 'at risk' learners. And Mike's summer baseball course has always had a full two-teacher partnership. While, in our long educational careers, these opportunities have been somewhat limited, these full partnership teaching experiences have been invaluable.

From our perspective, there are two main advantages in having two adult education teachers co-facilitate a course. The first is that there are two sets of eyes and ears observing the class. This has proven to be a tremendous tactical advantage in how the class is taught and how you can respond to certain situations that occur in your classroom. There have been times when one of the teachers misses certain subtle cues regarding the body language of students. In addition, having two educators in class has helped to plan lessons and course assignments based on these observations. A second advantage this model provides is that there is now the potential for two different perspectives to be brought into the class discussion. For example, when Mike is teaching his baseball class he brings a literature/theoretical view to the experiences as compared with his teaching colleague who brings a more practical/administrative one. These differences in perspectives add to the total learning experience for students and teachers alike.

We know that opportunities to teach with other adult educators are limited, but we believe that under some circumstances, this model can be utilized effectively.

Most of us will teach in situations where we will be alone with our students. However, the purpose of this chapter was to provide the new/inexperienced teacher with other ideas on how they may want to structure their class. Having others come into our classrooms to help teach can provide our students (and ourselves) with different perspectives and ideas. Also, using various co-teaching models can help us reflect on our craft. If you have the opportunity, give it a try. You may be surprised at the value of the experience.

Chapter 17:
Assessing Student Learning

How do we know that our students are learning? The history and philosophy of adult education provides us with more than one answer to this question. Even under the best circumstances, assessing student learning can be challenging. For students, it often conjures up negative images of their prior educational experiences. The learning environment you establish will help alleviate students' fears when it comes to evaluating their work. As a new teacher, you will no doubt find your first answers to these important questions within the program in which you are working.

In general, there are two basic types of assessments you can employ—formal and informal. If you are teaching traditional academic subjects or working in traditional settings (e.g. ABE/GED programs) you may find yourself using more standard/formal assessments. If your class work involves required academic subjects in a basic education or high school diploma program, there will probably be formal assessment resources available. If however, you are teaching an enrichment course in watercolor painting, or you are teaching academic/job training subjects in vocational education, it may be entirely possible that you may find yourself employing more informal assessment tools. Do not be deceived by the term "informal." Even informal assessments are valid means to accurately assess a student's progress. Joseph Moran (*Assessing Adult Learning: A Guide for Practitioners*, 2001) is an excellent resource for examining and implementing different assessment strategies, both informal and formal. Our goal is to provide you with basic strategies and guidelines to keep in mind if you are going to assess student learning in any venue. (In order to read more about assessment strategies with student writing see Chapter 11).

Four key questions come to mind when we think about assessing student learning in the context of adult education:

- Are the students returning to class and at least continuing their participation (in other words, are they dropping out)?

- Are they learning what they came to learn?

- Are they able to apply learning outside the classroom?

- Is what's going on in this class stimulating the desire on students' part to continue their learning?

Let's take each of these and briefly discuss them. Retention, obviously, is a big issue. One crystal clear indicator that students are not getting what they came for is for them to not return to your class. There's an old saying in this field: "Adults vote with their feet." To put it bluntly, if you have 15 students to begin your course but only 10 come back for the second class, you have a problem. You will most likely have to explain this attrition to the program director. It would be best to ask your 10 remaining people what they think is going on. Was the course description unclear? Did something we did during the first class or that is articulated in the course syllabus scare people away? We believe it is at this basic and foundational level—are students continuing to participate and show interest in your class?—where the assessment process begins.

But, of course, there are additional levels. Are students learning what they came to learn? Perhaps the best way to answer this question—and certainly the most direct—is to ask them. Talk to your students at various times during the course about their learning goals and what progress they are making toward achieving those goals. Perhaps ask them to write a minute paper or even a personal letter to you describing what they are learning. Asking your students about their learning will both provide you with important information and communicate an important message—that you *care* about their learning.

As we described earlier in this book (Chapter 2 and elsewhere), adults are practical learners. Therefore, it is critical that they be able to apply what they are learning in your class to outside problems and situations. Providing opportunities in the course plan for students to make these practical applications will go a long way toward ensuring meaningful learning is taking place. Allowing a little class time periodically to debrief the applicability of the course content may be a useful strategy for having your students think about how their learning connects to their world outside of class and having you learn the details of these applications. If the learning "works" in a useful manner in the lives of your students it is highly likely that you are succeeding in what you are doing inside the classroom.

Finally, we often judge the value of the learning experience by assessing the degree to which our teaching has stimulated students' further interest in learning the topic at hand. Have new questions emerged? Are people expressing excitement about carrying forward with their study? Is there a feeling that the course should not yet be ending? Sometimes the answers to these questions are not self-evident and are determined more or less intuitively. But there are other times when the evidence is clear and palpable. For example, we recently heard of a situation in a liberal arts course in a "Senior College" in Maine that consisted of 25 older learners (most of retirement age). These adult learners, upon reaching their eighth and final class in the semester, petitioned the school for a continuation of at least two more weeks of class with this instructor! When hunger for learning is piqued like this, there is little doubt that good and productive things are happening in the class.

A Few Suggestions

We have looked to our own practice as teachers and also have surveyed respected colleagues about their assessment practices. Here are some ideas we would like to share with you as you consider adopting your own assessment techniques.

- Consider involving your students in the design of a course project. Part of this design is to specify learning outcomes and ways to evaluate whether or not these outcomes have been achieved. If the student has been an active partner in this design, s/he will most likely participate enthusiastically in the assessment of learning. This type of partnership is, as we have written about in numerous places elsewhere in this book, an excellent way to practice adult education.

- Sometimes a test or quiz is used for assessment. Even though these words (along with a kindred one—"exam") are often avoided by adult educators because of the fear factor they invoke, they can be useful tools to evaluate what people know at a given time. While we usually consider tests to be high impact evaluations with serious implications (e.g., grades, diplomas, certificates, degrees, etc.), they may also be low-impact and even fun. Having students correct their own tests, or doing so in a dyad involving a classmate, can engage useful assessment of learning while also being a learning process in itself.

- As students leave class, they are asked to leave questions with the teacher to begin the next class. These questions provide benchmarks on how individual learning is progressing.

- At the end of class, each student shares with a classmate what they have learned that night. This self-assessment could first be written (in a "minute paper" or in some other format) and then shared verbally. In a small class, and especially once the group has met several times and the level of trust among individuals has developed, this exercise may even be tried with the class at-large.

- Peer assessment can be a powerful tool. As students present projects or an oral report in class, their peers provide a critique under the heading "Positive Hints."

- To help students recognize progress, use creative "pre-test" and "post-test" techniques.

- In some circumstances, you may want to have students create course portfolios. Portfolios can be an effective assessment tool that represents examples of the students' homework, various assignments/exercises, quizzes and even tests.

As a new teacher, you may find the use of one or more of these methods daunting. You may be saying to yourself, "Why all these approaches?"…What about the multiple choice and old-fashioned math tests I used to take in high school and college?… Aren't these the type of tests I should be administering?" The answer is "yes" and "no." There will be times when using a traditional exam as a major source of assessing learning is practical and necessary. However, over the past 20-30 years, adult education researchers have looked at ways in which assessment is changing. These are some of their conclusions.

- The way educators think about learning has changed; therefore the way students are assessed has also changed. Learners need to be actively engaged in the planning and facilitation of their own learning—and learning assessment. The greater the participation, the better.

- Educators are moving away from a norm-referenced system (e.g. Bell-curve student-to-student comparisons) to a criterion-referenced system. Criterion-referenced means that learning is based on a specific standard (e.g., the mastery of a certain level of knowledge or skill). In other words, now we are less interested in comparing or ranking students against each other and more interested in identifying the goal for learning and what successful achievement looks like.

- Society has changed. There is an ever-increasing need for adults to be independent, self-directed learners.

- More meaningful assessments tend towards looking at reliable evidence of learning needs. The educator focuses on looking for trends/patterns over time.

- Research shows that learning improves when descriptive feedback is given to students (as opposed to a simple letter or numeric grade). Providing a narrative evaluation admittedly takes more time and energy than simply marking the letter "B" or the number "87" on a paper or project. But a narrative-based assessment is often infinitely more beneficial to the learner.

- Assessment is most effective when it reflects an understanding of learning as multidimensional, integrated, and revealed in performance over time.

- Assessment requires attention to outcomes but also and equally to the experience and process that leads to those outcomes.

- Assessment works best when it is ongoing, not episodic.

The ongoing nature of assessment leads us to also suggest that evaluating student learning—in the best case—involves multiple indicators. In her acclaimed book, *Making Classroom Assessment Work*, Anne Davies writes convincingly about sources of evidence. Davies claims that there are three general sources of assessment evidence gathered in classrooms: *observations* of learning, *products* students create, and *conversations* (e.g., discussing learning with students). When evidence is collected from these three sources over time, trends and patterns become apparent.

Observations may include: classroom presentations, reading aloud, group activities, sharing opinions in class, asking questions, non-verbal communication, expressions of interest or enthusiasm, and just about anything a teacher might see students do in class. These observations may or may not be formally recorded (note: it takes time and discipline to record these data). But the information we collect through our eyes during our face-to-face engagements with students can be and often are indicative of what and how they are learning.

Teachers also collect evidence through student work. These may include papers, notebooks, tests/quizzes, homework assignments, and portfolios. The thoughtful adult education teacher often tries to give an element of choice to students in what form products may take. For example, invite students to show their learning by drawing a diagram, making a timeline, telling a story, designing a web page, filming a video, building a model, or creating a collage. Allowing products to express both left-brain (logical, linear) and right-brain (creative, intuitive) activities encourages whole-person learning. It also enhances the enjoyment for the learner and teacher (since you get to experience a variety of expressions).

Finally, assessment is enabled substantially by having conversations with students about their learning. The conversation may be face-to-face (e.g., individually or even as part of a group conversation) or in writing. Oral conversations with students may take place during class time or outside of class. We have learned from experience that the best conversations often occur during breaks or before and after class when students may be feeling more relaxed. Written conversations may take place through a dialog journal, memorandum, personal letter, or through email communication.

When we listen to students in this way, we invite them to think about their own learning. As Anne Davies says, "As they think and explain, we can gather evidence about what they know and understand. We can find out what they did or what they created…what was difficult or easy, what they might do differently next time, and what risks they take as learners" (Davies, 2000, p. 39).

If You Must Test!

Both authors prefer to use assessments other than formal testing. However, we understand that a test or quiz may be required in some adult education contexts. While our experience is limited (in giving tests, not taking them!), we would like to offer a set of guidelines if indeed your situation requires you to plan and administer formal tests to your adult students.

- Make the first test relatively easy. Research on motivation indicates that early success in a course increases students' motivation and confidence. Students who do well on an initial exam tend to improve their grades on subsequent exams.

- Test multiple times. One test tends to put inordinate pressure on students. Giving two or more exams throughout a course spreads out the stress, allows students to concentrate on one chunk of material at a time, and allows both the student and teacher to monitor progress.

- No surprises! Giving a "pop" quiz or otherwise surprising your students with an unannounced formal assessment is bad practice. It is disrespectful and will usually result in anger, resentment, and maybe even resistance.

- Encourage students to study in groups. They will learn from one another and not feel so isolated. Group study is often also a good community building tool.

- Ask students how you can help them become better prepared for the test. You want your students to succeed, right? So give them the tools to succeed (in addition to teaching the information that will be the basis for the test). Is there a difficult content area that needs review? Is there a barrier in the classroom itself that may be easily removed in order to increase comfort and the ability to concentrate (e.g., a light that is missing, a distracting noise, etc.)?

- Give practice exams. This helps students gauge what is expected of them. You can use practice exams as the basis for review sessions or student study groups.

- Allow students to evaluate the exam. If you want a sense of how students felt about the exam, ask them to complete an unsigned evaluation form that poses questions such as: Did the content you expected to see appear on this exam? Were the questions clear? What questions, if any, confused you? Assessing the assessment tool is an empowering experience for students and will also be a useful learning experience for you as you plan future examinations.

- Debrief. We firmly believe that assessments ought to be learning experiences in themselves. Papers, projects, portfolios, and other non-exam assessments are "learning rich" experiences for most students. This is not usually the case with tests or quizzes. But you can help to transform a test or quiz into a learning experience by debriefing it after the test has been administered (but don't wait too long—the principle of recency is important here).

Examples of Assessments Used by Adult Education Practitioners

Now we would like to offer several specific examples. We start with a basic, somewhat traditional system used to evaluate written work. The following exhibit is from a Business English class. The goal of this course is to help students learn how to improve written communication in business settings. Towards this goal, they are expected to learn proper letter/memo formatting, style, tone, grammar, and punctuation. As students write various types of business correspondence, they are assessed using the following rubric ("Rubric" is a common term used in education that describes the categories on how student work is evaluated):

Business English Writing Evaluation

The following factors are used in evaluating written assignments: Formatting, spelling, punctuation, grammar, writing strategy and tone/style. Each paper handed in is assigned a value of 100 points. Points are deducted from the work based on errors in the above areas. Papers receiving a grade of 80 or higher are satisfactory. Points are deducted as follows:

Factors	Points deducted
Formatting	2 points per error (6 maximum)
Spelling	3 points (9 max.)
Punctuation	2 points (6 max.)
Grammar	2 points (8 max.)
Appropriate Strategy	2 points (4 max.)
Tone/Style	2 points (4 max.)

This evaluation system is designed to help students understand the importance of using effective and proper communication skills in the workplace. Evaluated student work is returned with suggestions about how to improve their writing. In addition, students are encouraged to re-write work to gain a better understanding of proper business writing techniques. In some

Exhibit 17-1

instances, when it is clear that the student did not have a clear understanding of certain guidelines, work is resubmitted for a new evaluation. Note that a baseline for satisfactory work is established without the use of traditional (A, B, C, etc.) grades.

Now let's take a look at a series of assessments used in teaching mathematics. The purpose of using only one subject for the following exhibits is to provide you with different evaluative approaches in connection with that subject. Remember—there are multiple approaches that may be used to assess student learning.

In the following exhibit, the teacher uses journal writing to help the student gain insights about their feelings before and after taking the course. This strategy uses a qualitative approach and is designed to help the student *reflect* on their learning experience.

Math Journal

Exhibit 17-2

Name: Date:
Place an "x" on the line below to represent how you felt about math entering this course.

Hate math   Scared of math   Math's OK   Like math   Love math

Now place an "x" on the line below to represent how you felt about math leaving this course.

Hate math   Scared of math   Math's OK   Like math   Love math

If your feelings changed, please discuss what helped change them.
1. How did the journal process work for you? How would you evaluate your journal work?
2. How did the structure of the class influence your learning? (Group lessons vs. individualized work?)
3. In what areas of math did you have the greatest growth? What areas still could use improvement?
4. How would you evaluate your computer skills? (*For this particular class, use of specific computer applications, e.g., Excel, was required*)

The above example of a student-centered critical self-evaluative approach helps learners to understand how their feelings may have changed in relation to the course. Because math is a subject that often involves traditional examinations, this kind of assessment recognizes that a learner's accomplishment can be expressed in an alternative way.

The next example is an assessment tool that involves a project. Math teachers often use project work to help students develop critical thinking skills. Exhibit 17-3 provides a rubric for a math project.

Scoring Rubric for Math Project

Exhibit 17-3

Score/points	Presentation	Graph/chart	Written analysis
4	Presentation is clear, concise & soundly supported. The presenter clearly convinces the audience of the findings.	Student demonstrates at least two graphs studied this semester. Visuals are properly labeled, correctly identified as to its shape & if linear, a correct formula is found.	A clear position is identified & supported. The written analysis is thoroughly complete in following the 7 steps in the guideline. There are correct & in-depth conclusions to the graph. Presentation is clear
3	& supported. The presenter convinces the audience of the findings.	Student demonstrates one graph studied this semester. Visuals are somewhat labeled, correctly identified as to its shape & if linear, the formula may not be correct.	A clear position is identified & partially supported. The analysis addresses the 7 steps on guidelines but not as thoroughly. There are correct conclusions to the graphs.
2	Presentation lacks clarity & is partially supported. The presenter somewhat convinces the audience of the findings.	Student uses a bar or circle graph for visual. If chooses graph studied, student labels incorrectly. The shape or formula may be incorrect.	The identified position lacks clarity and its partially supported. The analysis somewhat follows the 7 steps. There may be incorrect analysis of the graphs.

| 1 | Presentation lacks focus & is unclear. The presenter is ambiguous with the findings. | No graph or visual is given or if present, lacking in identifying shape or formula. | The identified position is unclear and does not address the 7 steps. Analysis of graphs is missing or incorrect. |

Exhibit 17-3 demonstrates a clear, well-defined rubric for evaluating student project work. When evaluating projects, having clear objectives is critical for enhancing the learning experience. As you compare the differences between Exhibit 17-2 and 17-3, remember that both approaches have value in assessing student learning. The key question you need to ask yourself is, "What approach can I use in assessing student learning that will provide the most meaning for everyone—both student and teacher?"

Of course, we hope you will use a variety of approaches in assessing your students.

The final exhibit provides a sample of assessing portfolio work for an Algebra course. Use of student portfolios is a common method of student learning in adult education programs. Here is what a teacher said about assessing portfolios in her class.

"The variety of approaches I get from students is as varied as their personalities. For example, one student took each chapter, discussed her strengths and weaknesses, and then made a connection to life skill applications. These included working on a quilt…to analyzing a complex set of data on homelessness and questioning that data with newly acquired Algebra knowledge. Another student looked at each chapter as an "era" in her life and how she was affected by it. These portfolios are powerful documentations of a student's journey in learning, not just mathematics, but reflecting on who they are as a learner. The best part of the portfolio process is having the students share their portfolios with one another."

—Pam Meader

Exhibit 17-4 provides assessment guidelines for a math portfolio. For some students it may involve only one course of study while for others it may involve several. The key component of the assessment involves the student's active reflection on their work.

Exhibit 17-4

Portfolio Self-Assessment (Algebra Part A)

You will soon complete Algebra Part A. For some of you, this has been your first math class with Dover Adult Education. For others, it also includes courses in Math Concepts, Consumer Math, and/or Math Basics. As you reflect on the class (or classes) you have taken, think about what you knew coming into the course and what you know now. Your portfolio should be a reflection of this journey. Many colleges are now requiring portfolios as proof of knowledge gained. As you create your portfolio, pretend that you are designing your presentation to show to a college admissions person.

Think About:

1. What skills have you acquired that you feel are important for either college or the workplace?

2. Where have you demonstrated analytical skills (e.g., interpreting results in terms of the real world, relating results to other problems, relating problems to your own life experiences)?

3. How could you demonstrate critical thinking skills that indicate:

- A variety of problem solving techniques using visual, written, and manipulatives.

- Taking a problem and going further, a "what if" approach.

- What areas of algebra do you feel you have mastered or are your strengths?

- What areas of algebra do you feel inadequate in and that require more study?

- What areas of algebra have you actually applied outside the classroom either at work, as a community member, or at home?

Think about these questions as you create your portfolio. All I require is an introductory page whose purpose is to explain how and why you organized your portfolio and your self-assessment. The rest of the portfolio is your creation.

Summary

In this chapter we have presented you with a set of ideas about assessment followed by specific examples of non-traditional and creative assessment tools being used by experienced adult educators today. One reason we deliberately focused on mathematics in the exemplars was because many people believe math is an area where only traditional assessments (e.g., tests and quizzes) can be administered. As you can see, experienced teachers of adults use various and creative assessments to determine how and what students are learning. As a new teacher, we suggest that you work closely with your program administrator so you can learn what assessments are typically used in your subject area and what tools may already be available to you. Then, as your experience and confidence grows, we encourage you to expand your own assessment portfolio into some of the other areas described in this chapter and elsewhere in *The New Teacher of Adults*.

Chapter 18:
The Quest for Continuous Improvement

The true mark of an excellent teacher is not necessarily one who receives great acclaim from students, whose learners all pass examinations with honors, or even one who is remembered fondly years after s/he has retired from the classroom. In our view we cannot be deemed excellent, whether we are new teachers or have years of experience, unless we admit that no matter what our achievements have been we still have more to learn and ways to improve our craft. Remember the core principle that we have communicated throughout this book: The adult educator needs to always be a learner. Learning about ourselves as teachers is just as important as learning about the subject matter that we instruct.

This chapter is designed to help you think about and improve your perform-ance as a teacher of adults. Some of the practices we shall describe will seem obvious to you while others may not. Several will be more challenging to employ than others. We have organized this chapter into three sections: (1) Methods you can use alone (2) Receiving feedback from students (3) Getting by with a little help from your friends.

Methods You Can Use Alone

The key to improving as a teacher is reflection. We have already shared thoughts in this book about the power of *journal writing* as a reflective prac-tice. While journals are often a useful tool for learning among students, it is also useful for teachers. One way to become more closely in touch with your own practice as a teacher is to take time immediately after class to jot down your thoughts. Write brief reflections on the following prompts: What went especially well this evening? Why did it go so well? What did not go as well as I would have liked or had planned? Why? If I could change one thing about the way I taught this evening's class it would be…It is important to write such reflections as soon after the conclusion of your class as possible because of the ability to remember details. (E.g., Mike tends to write his jour-nal entries early in the morning so will usually wait 8-10 hours after the conclusion of an evening class to write such a reflection. This is about the longest we recommend you going between the experience and the written reflection. Allen, on the other hand, will jot down reflective notes almost immediately after his night class because he tends to forget.) Getting into the habit of spending even as few as five minutes writing thoughtfully about your recent teaching practice will not only help you to celebrate your successes and focus attention on weaknesses but over time will increase your general self-awareness as a teacher.

One of the best ways to learn about yourself is to *videotape* a class in whole or in part. In our own teaching practice videotaping has long been a crucial method of obtaining feedback. Most adult education programs will either own its own video camera or have easy access to one. Mounting the camera on a tripod, placing it in a corner of the classroom out of the way of students, inserting a blank tape, and turning the camera to "record" requires an investment of only a few minutes. The return on this small investment can be remarkable.

Videotaping can show you aspects of your teaching practice that most human providers of feedback, for example your students and/or colleague observers, will usually fail to record. You will hear how fast or slowly you speak and how clearly. You will see gestures the way students see them and can determine for yourself how "natural" they appear and also how well your physical movements complement the message you are trying to communicate. Habits that you may be completely unaware of will reveal themselves. For example, one time when Mike viewed a videotape of himself teaching he noticed that he had a habit of touching his mustache when students were talking, an eccentricity that never once came up in decades of reading student evaluations. You will hear students' questions and observe how directly and clearly you answer them. If your videotape includes a class discussion you will be able to observe how many verbal interventions you made (you can even count them!), whether or not you cut off a student's comments, and how well the discussion stayed on track. Admittedly it's not always easy, at least at first, to teach in a completely natural and unaffected manner when you look up and see the little red light glowing on the video camera in the back corner of your classroom. But take heart— the presence of the camera usually fades to oblivion after only a few minutes. It is also not easy, once you arrive home with your video-tape, to sit down and watch yourself on television. But the benefits of engaging this simple and easily accessible technology can be legion.

A less powerful yet nonetheless useful way of obtaining feedback about your teaching is to *audiotape* all or part of a class. Here you will have verbal but not visual data. We actually got into the practice of frequently tape recording our teaching because of student requests to record a class they had to miss. Recording technology of all sorts—standard cassette sized machines, "micro" cassettes, and some of the more advanced cell phones and other communication devices— are ubiquitous and easy to use. While we do not necessarily recommend video or audio taping every class, doing so once or twice a semester will provide you with valuable information on which to build as a continuously improving teacher.

One additional method that does not require the assistance of other human beings is worthy of note. On occasion Allen has used a process in which he *writes a letter to his future self* that describes how he would like to be as a teacher in three or five years. Although it's not something people are always comfortable talking about we believe that every person has both a real and an ideal self-image as a spouse, parent, worker, citizen, etc. Although we may not phrase it exactly this way, "Who am I?" and "Who would I like to become?" are questions human beings continually ask themselves. (Personal self-assessment is especially prevalent at the start of each new calendar year in the context of making resolutions, in religious times of reflection and atonement such as Lent and Yom Kippur, on birthdays and anniversaries, etc.) Taking the time once a year to write a letter to the teacher you would like to become in the future can be a fruitful expression of this natural tendency to seek and find an ideal self.

Receiving Feedback from Students

This is one of the most common ways teachers learn how they are doing as adult education facilitators. Few if any adult education courses (or even half-day workshops) end without a paper and pencil evaluation form being completed by participants. Most often this instrument will invite learners to rate their degree of satisfaction vis-à-vis achieving their personal or professional goals and the style and perceived competence of the teacher. While sometimes these evaluations are derisively referred to as "Happiness Ratings," we do not condemn end-of-course paper and pencil instruments that mostly measure satisfaction because, as we have stated over and over in this book, we believe it is important for students to be happy! But a once per course assessment is the minimum standard for which you should reach.

We know of many colleagues who check the pulse of their students with a paper and pencil evaluation at the mid-way point in a course as well as at the end. (Note: Most adult education programs will require an end-of-course student evaluation while a mid-course assessment is usually voluntary and teacher initiated.) This kind of "formative evaluation" can go a long way toward helping the teacher understand how s/he is doing, whether students feel their goals are being met, and levels of satisfaction with the readings, lectures, and other aspects of the curriculum. If done mid-way through a course and problems are exposed there is time to correct them. Some teachers we know prefer to conduct mid-course reviews orally, for example by taking the last 10 minutes of the class in the middle of the term to provide feedback. Other teachers prefer to keep this mid-course review written and anonymous. It is also possible to combine the anonymity and focus group-type synergy that often derives from group discussion by you, the teacher, leaving the room and having the class talk about their opinions of the course with one or two students assigned to report the results to you. In the chapter in which we discuss the art and science of lectures, we provide an example of an evaluation instrument (see Exhibit 8-2). This, or any variation thereof, could be adapted for use as either a mid-term or end-of course-evaluation.

The adult education scholar Stephen Brookfield and his colleague Stephen Preskill, in their book *Discussion as a Way of Teaching*, recommend yet another way of continuously obtaining feedback. (Please see "Sources for Further Reading" for details about this book.) They call it the "Critical Incident Questionnaire" (CIQ). CIQ is a simple classroom evaluation tool that may be used to find out what and how students are learning. It consists of a single sheet of paper containing five questions, all of which focus on critical moments or actions that have taken place in the class (as judged by the learners.) The five questions are pre-printed on a page of paper such that there is ample blank space beneath each question for students to write down their thoughts. The CIQ is handed out to learners a few minutes before the end of class. (Brookfield and Preskill recommend doing this after every class, but we believe that the frequency of administration of the CIQ may vary depend on circumstances. They also recommend using carbon paper between pages so each student may keep a copy of her/his comments. However we feel that this practice may also be exempted without losing much of the effectiveness of the CIQ as a feedback tool.)

The five questions in the CIQ are always the same:

1. At what moment in class this week were you most engaged as a learner?

2. At what moment in class this week were you most distanced as a learner?

3. What action taken (by anyone) did you find most affirming or helpful?

4. What action taken (by anyone) did you find most puzzling or confusing?

5. What surprised you most about class this week?

It is very important that the CIQ remain anonymous. In fact, we write simple instructions at the top of the page that expressly asks students not to write their name. The next part of the process is very important. The adult education teacher reads the CIQs and takes notes on the key ideas and experiences that have been reported. If you have the time and energy you may wish to type these notes up for distribution. What is not voluntary is reporting the main ideas of the last CIQ at the start of the next class session. We usually do this only orally. Then invite responses and discussion of the comments.

This is not an easy process to undertake. Sometimes students' comments can be severe and may even be taken personally. However, engaging the CIQ process on a regular basis is one of the best ways to build a strong and consistent feedback cycle into your teaching. Also, as Brookfield and Preskill write, it helps the teacher "explain that we're trying to earn the right to ask students to think and speak critically by first modeling this in front of them. The overall effect is often very powerful, particularly when students see us putting ourselves in the uncomfortable position of highlighting comments that show us in a bad light." (Brookfield and Preskill, 2005, p. 51) Over time use of the CIQ will help you, the new teacher of adults, learn a great deal about your own teaching. It will also help you to earn the right to ask your students to take some of the same risks in their learning that you have modeled by virtue of undertaking this powerful process.

Finally, months after you finish a course you may wish to speak to students with whom you have stayed in touch in order to get feedback about their experiences in your classroom. This approach is helpful because your former students are in a better position to be honest with you and also have the advantage of having some distance between the experience itself and talking with you about it such as to create a more balanced perspective. We have found these after-the-fact conversations with students to be especially candid and useful.

Getting By With A Little Help From Your Friends

This final strategy for continuously improving your teaching relies on obtaining the assistance of a colleague. Invite a fellow teacher or program administrator to visit your class and observe your teaching. Some adult education directors will do this anyway as part of the faculty review process. But being proactive and intentionally designing a colleague-observation as a learning (as compared with an evaluation) experience could greatly benefit you.

Here are a few simple procedures to keep in mind when planning a peer observation:

1. Give your colleague observer plenty of advanced notice.

2. Provide a copy of your course syllabus to your colleague in advance of the observation so s/he can see the overall scope of the course as well as the agenda you have planned for the specific class to be observed.

3. Ask your colleague to focus on areas that you are most concerned about in your teaching. Do you feel your lectures are too dry? That you lose control of group discussion? That you need to work on the way you respond to students' questions? Specifically ask your colleague to focus attention on several areas where you are most interested in obtaining feedback. (If you

do not do this there is a risk that the feedback you receive will be overly generalized and not very useful.)

4. Before the two of you commit to doing this peer observation be sure your colleague is willing to write notes after the observation and to take time to debrief the experience you.

5. When the day arrives when this peer observation takes place be sure to introduce your colleague to the members of your class. It is best to be honest with your students and, in addition to acknowledging the new person's presence in the room, perhaps say something like "Mary is with us tonight to observe the way I teach and to provide me with feedback. We do this for one another and have found it to be a wonderful way to grow as teachers." Such a simple and direct statement of purpose should quiet any fears on the part of your students that they are being evaluated or that something is wrong.

6. After the peer observation has been concluded and you have listened to your colleague's feedback, don't be afraid to change. Even if you only alter one small practice your willingness to change what you do as a teacher demonstrates the efficacy of peer observation as a valid professional development tool. Additionally, letting your colleague know that you have made a change based on her/his observation and feedback validates the entire process and makes everyone more enthusiastic about engaging peer feedback in the future.

Teaching is a complex and challenging activity and one that becomes more robust and rewarding as we grow in its artistry. The ideas we have discussed in this chapter should help you to obtain feedback and engage the kind of professional and personal reflection that will enable you to continuously grow in this supple and splendid craft.

Chapter 19:
Ten Things to Remember

We hope you have found value in this book and that you have identified tools and suggestions to use for your first (and maybe second, and even third) teaching experience. Nobody teaches on a social, emotional, or academic "island." Each of us is influenced by, and is a product of, the many and varied roles we have played and continue to play in life: student, spouse, parent, friend, worker, and citizen. Each of these roles teaches us; consequently we bring this lifetime of learning as our most important tool into the classroom.

In some ways, every time we enter a class we are all new teachers. Every time we go through the classroom door to teach, we enter the undiscovered, fraught with new and exciting challenges. We have listed some ideas that all teachers may want to keep in mind, attempting to provide additional guidance and support. On the surface, some of these may not appear to be practical suggestions; but as you start to teach, we believe you will fine sound advice and perhaps even some solace.

The first five minutes of class is critical. The tone you set in the first few minutes often determines how the class will go. Take advantage of this special time. Get your students' attention; use effective exercises to keep the learning momentum going. Remember, you will set the tone for how the class will go. Don't be afraid to lead.

Practice patience and forgiveness. Over time, you will appreciate these two qualities. Your ability to be patient will help not only you, but also your students. Not everyone learns at the same pace or the same way. Some students have been away from school a long time, and they will be scared and apprehensive. It will take time for them to get re-acclimated, so be patient.

Parker Palmer, a noted educator, once said that one of the critical characteristics teachers can take into the classroom with them is the capacity to forgive. Our students will make mistakes, not always show up, and sometimes be very difficult to deal with. Be prepared to forgive.

Progress not perfection... be prepared to make mistakes. In conjunction with patience and forgiveness is the idea that we should focus on progress, not necessarily perfection. You expect your students to make mistakes. Guess what? You will, too. Perfection can be a goal you set, but it can sometimes be an illusion and rarely accomplished. Focus on how both you and your students' progress, not the lack of perfection. If you use "progress not perfection" as a learning motto, maybe everyone can relax a little and enjoy their learning journey a bit more.

Listen to your students. Do you remember when you were a student and you felt that the teacher wasn't listening to you? Take that into account when you engage students in dialogue. Students will listen better if they believe you are listening. Set the example.

Don't use red ink! This is one of the cardinal rules of adult education. Red ink conjures up negative memories for adult students. As you review and grade papers, remember to use *any* color but red when commenting on and marking student papers. Use colored stars, happy faces if you wish, anything but red ink.

Learn how to balance challenging vs. supporting your students. The approach you use to challenge students versus the need to support them in their learning is the crux of the "art" of teaching. As you gain experience, you will better understand the dynamics involved in balancing how you will emotionally support students and appropriately challenge them at the same time. Every student is different, and your need to make adjustments to this balancing act will take effort, creativity, tact, and even guile. It truly is the essence of the art of teaching.

Criticize in private, praise in public. No one likes to hear negative things expressed in a public setting. Remember how teachers used to do that in middle and high school classes? It is demeaning and a sure recipe for disaster for both you and your students. If you criticize in public expect dropouts.

Conversely, students like to hear good things about themselves. Praise solid efforts and work, and share it with the class. Don't be surprised if at first, those students who are recognized for their fine work react in quiet and even non-responsive ways. They probably have never been in a situation where they have been praised in public before. Don't get frustrated. They'll get used to it and begin to exhibit positive reactions.

The essence of teaching is creating "relationships." Building relationships is what teaching is all about. Let us clarify this statement. We try to build relationships between the subject we teach and our students. In doing this, we help students to discover how the content is relevant to their lives. We build relationships with our students. This, of course, is the foundation to sound teaching. Hopefully, over time, students build a learning community, a community of learners if you will, with their fellow students. When this happens, your job as teacher takes on new and even more exciting forms.

When in doubt, bring food. We learned this from our friend and colleague Will Callender. Adult learners like to be fed. Food can be a wonderful catalyst for bringing well-needed informality to the classroom. For example, food can be used effectively to help make people comfortable in the first class. Candy, fruit, or even pastries are popular selections.

Know your students' names! Nothing creates a comfortable and welcoming learning environment more than knowing the names of your students. This is not always an easy task, especially if you have a large classroom. Nameplates or nametags can do wonders for helping everyone get acquainted and more comfortable with each other.

Enjoy your time teaching. We have found it to be a rewarding profession. However, we know that most of you reading this book may be teaching part-time, maybe for the first time. We hope you find the same fulfillment and excitement we have found in our many years of working with adult learners.

For us, teaching goes beyond a mere job—it is a joy. It transcends typical concepts of "work" and even enters a mystical arena where we realize that we are engaged in one of the most important activities we humans do. We have also learned that while we are offering our knowledge and skill to help other people to learn and grow, there are times when we learn and grow even more than our students. In short, teaching adults is a wonderful experience! As a new teacher of adults, we hope you enjoy your initial experience—and have many more thereafter.

Sources for Further Learning

Throughout this book we have made reference to a variety of sources that we have found useful both in our teaching and in the writing of *The New Teacher of Adults*. Here are those source materials, and several additional ones, with brief annotations. These books are listed in chronological order by date of publication.

If You Want to Write
Brenda Ueland
Gray Wolf Press (1936)

This book has been around a long time and has served as the inspiration for many later texts about the art and craft of writing. The famous American poet Carl Sandburg called *If You Want to Write* the best book ever written on this topic. The author is an unabashed "cheerleader" for you to write with originality and spirit. Many readers walk away from reading this with renewed enthusiasm for their own writing practice. While some of the stories and examples used in this book will sound "old fashioned" to the contemporary reader (it was, after all, written during the Great Depression), there are gifts and qualities in these pages that transcend time.

The Meaning of Adult Education
Lindeman, Eduard C.
Harvest House Ltd. (1961)

This book, originally written in the early part of the 20th Century but reissued in 1961, is considered a seminal work in the field of adult education. While primarily a book describing the philosophical underpinnings of adult education, Lindeman argues convincingly at the end of *The Meaning of Adult Education* for the use of discussion as the best way for adults to teach and learn. The author is highly quotable and readers of this book often say how they find themselves underlining nearly every page. We highly recommend *The Meaning of Adult Education* to anyone who is interested in exploring the foundations of this field of practice.

The Skillful Teacher
Brookfield, Stephen D.
Jossey-Bass (1990)

This book, written by a well-known professor of adult education, can serve as an excellent introductory resource for the new teacher. Brookfield focuses on practical methods and includes useful guidelines for lecturing, facilitating discussions, using simulations and role-play, giving helpful evaluations, overcoming resistance to learning, and dealing with special problems in teaching. Although he is an academic the author is highly readable and does a nice job mixing research findings with practical advice.

Education for Judgment: The Art of Discussion Leadership
Edited by Roland Christensen, David Garvin, and Ann Sweet
Harvard Business School Press (1991)

This is one of the best books we have ever read about facilitating discussions. The Harvard Business School is renowned for its use of the case discussion method of teaching and learning. Many of the contributing authors to this book are experienced teachers in that program. *Education for Judgment* consists of 17 essays—some more theoretical and others more practical in nature—about the various joys and challenges of discussion facilitation.

Help Yourself: How to take advantage of your learning styles.
Sonbuchner, Gail Murphy
New Readers Press (1991)

This is an excellent resource to discover both your learning style and the learning styles of your students. This practical handbook provides you with a step-by-step method of learning how you (and your students) learn. The book goes further and helps you understand how your style relates to organization and time management, memory, listening, reading and reading comprehension, writing, mathematics, and even test taking. This is an essential book for the new teacher who wants to understand how adults learn and how learning styles can influence teaching.

Tools for Teaching
Barbara Davis
Jossey-Bass (1993)

This is a large (430 pages) manual that very much fulfills the promise of its title. Barbara Davis offers a large range of specific tools to help the classroom teacher. There are thorough sections (each including 3 or more specific chapters) on themes such as responding to a diverse student body, discussion strategies, lecture strategies, writing and homework assignments, and evaluation to improve teaching. *Tools for Teaching* is easy to read and each chapter ends with a rich set of references. Although this book is now somewhat dated—especially the parts that deal with media and technology—it would still make an excellent addition to the adult education teacher's bookshelf.

If You Can Talk, You Can Write.
Saltzman, Joel
Warner Books, Inc. (1993)

This is a fun, insightful, "blue-collar" handbook on writing. The author takes you through a series of suggestions designed to improve writing style and get you writing. Chapters cover such topics as overcoming procrastination and ways to get started, the technique of talking on paper, choosing topics to write on, the value of writing and rewriting, and basic suggestions and ideas to remember as you write. Many chapters include a series of fun exercises and "pop quizzes" designed to build confidence along with a variety of interesting quotes from writers, musicians and philosophers.

The Tao of Teaching
Nagel, G.
Primus/Donald L. Fine (1994)

The author links the ancient Chinese book of wisdom, *The Tao Te Ching*, to modern teaching practice. Organized into 81 brief chapters, each a meditation on one of the tenets of Taoism, this book treats many core aspects of teaching. We find the quotations at the beginning of each chapter that serves as that chapter's theme to be especially refreshing: "Tranquility is more important than perfection;" "Do not try to rule through cleverness;" "Know one's own roots to embrace others." While most of the examples the author uses come from primary and secondary education, the adult education practitioner will find many opportunities to use and benefit from this book.

Becoming a Critically Reflective Teacher
Brookfield, S. D.
Jossey-Bass (1995)

This could be considered a sequel to the author's 1990 book. This text provides an in-depth discussion of what critical reflection is, how it works, and methods to achieve it. Specific tools are offered including learning autobiographies, seeing yourself through the students' eyes, working with "at risk" students, use of critical incident questionnaires, and looking at the theory and practice of critical reflection from many different perspectives.

The Winning Trainer
Eitington, Julius E.
Gulf Publishing Co. (1996)

The specific audience of this book is the corporate trainer. However, it can also be used as an excellent reference tool for adult education classroom teachers. It contains ideas for getting a class started including icebreakers, a variety of ideas for small group learning, role-playing, different types of games and simulations, and problem solving exercises. In addition, *The Winning Trainer* provides team building ideas and exercises, methods of lecture, and tools for student-based evaluation of the course. This is an applied handbook designed to help give you ideas on how to create learning teams in your classroom. While its orientation is corporate based, this book can serve as a reference and resource for new ideas.

The Courage to Teach
Palmer, Parker
Jossey-Bass (1998)

This book, written by a well-known contemporary educator and consultant, takes the reader on an emotional and spiritual journey on why we teach. Palmer effectively discusses the importance of learning environments, developing a sense of connectedness between teacher and student, issues of identity and integrity, fears and barriers, and the creation of teaching/learning communities. This is expressly not a "methods" book as the author believes and argues in these pages that the source of good teaching is "the human heart."

The Right to Write
Julia Cameron
Jeremy P. Tarcher/Putnam (1998)

We consider this a more contemporary "sibling" of the Brenda Ueland book on writing. Julia Cameron, who has also written several famous books about creativity, shares her strong humanistic philosophy as she gives words of encouragement to the reader. Especially useful are the "Initiation Tools" provided at the end of each chapter. These are exercises that invite the reader to practice an idea or principle that has been discussed earlier.

Teaching with the Internet: Lessons from the Classroom
Leu, Donald and Leu, Deborah Diadiun
Christopher-Gordon Publisher, Inc. Norwood, MA (1999)

This is an applied guide for teachers thinking about using the Internet in their teaching. The book focuses on how to teach effectively using the Internet. Its primary audience is public school teachers but it can be adapted for use by adult educators in ABE, GED, High School Diploma, or job training programs. This book provides four instructional models (workshop, activity, project, and inquiry) to use the Internet in the classroom. It covers diverse teaching tips in areas of using the Internet, navigation strategies, communicating with email and mailing lists, exploring various sites, instructional strategies and examining Internet use in such disciplines as English, Social Studies, Science, and Mathematics.

Making Classroom Assessment Work
Anne Davies
Connections Publishing (2000)

Davies makes a core distinction between assessment (the ongoing collection of information about student progress that helps to inform teaching) and evaluation (a judgment about whether or not students have achieved goals). In this small book—it is less than 90 pages—the author guides the teacher through a process of using classroom assessment as a tool. Numerous samples and stories help to ground this book in reality and enhances its usefulness.

Equipped for the Future Content Standards
Sondra Stein
National Institute for Literacy (2000)

Equipped for the Future (EFF) is a collaborative, multi-year standards initiative in adult literacy. This book, which is subtitled "What Adults Need to Know and Be Able to Do in the 21st Century," provides details about EFF standards, how they work, and information about teaching and learning within the EFF framework. Specific examples provide detailed case studies showing how teachers have used a wide range of EFF tools to build learner competence. This source book may be obtained free of charge by contacting the National Institute for Literacy in Washington, D.C.

Assessing Adult Learning: A Guide for Practitioners
Joseph Moran
Krieger Publishing Co. (2001)

This is a good resource to help understand the intricacies of assessment. Moran makes a major distinction between formal and informal assessments, e.g. informal assessments do not rely on published materials and standardized procedures but depend on the creativity of educators to develop appropriate and authentic ways to evaluate and improve learning. The author provides readers with practical guidelines for designing relevant tests, making the most of test results, mastering performance portfolios, and applying assessment strategies in adult education.

Teaching with Fire: Poetry That Sustains the Courage to Teach
Edited by Sam Intrator and Megan Scribner
Jossey-Bass (2003)

This book is different than most in this list of resources because it is not a practical or applied text. It is an inspirational one. It consists of 88 poems, some famous and others not, that have been selected by 88 teachers across the United States as poems that have inspired their craft. The book is designed such that side by side (on opposite pages) are the poem itself and a brief essay written by the teacher who selected it reflecting on how and why this poem has been an influential force in her/his life and work.

Collaborating Online: Learning Together in Community
Palloff, R. and Pratt, K.
Jossey-Bass (2005)

This book is designed to help online teachers be more creative in engaging their students to work with one another. It has four sections: An overview of online collaboration, special challenges, assessment and evaluation of collaborative work, and 13 specific ways teachers can encourage collaboration (e.g., use of simulations, jigsaw activities, fishbowls, etc.)

Discussion as a Way of Teaching (2nd Edition)
Brookfield, S. D. and Preskill, S.
Jossey-Bass (2005)

Subtitled "Tools and Techniques for Democratic Classrooms," *Discussion As A Way of Teaching* is dedicated entirely to exploring and art and science of discussion facilitation in educational settings. We consider this to be an important resource if you are interested in learning more about the use of discussion facilitation methods of instruction. It provides a blend of theoretical and practical advice on issues such as preparation, keeping discussion going through questioning, and discussion in diverse settings. The second edition also includes a section on discussion facilitation in an online environment.

Teaching Tips: Strategies, Research, and Theory for College and University Teachers
Wilbert McKeachie
Houghton Mifflin (2006)

This book, currently in its 12th edition, has been remarkably successful as a basic primer for college teachers. While it integrates research findings from psychology, education, and other salient disciplines, the tone is very much a "how to" manual. The titles of the book's six sections, each of which includes several chapters, will give you a feel for the content: Getting Started, Basic Skills For Facilitating Student Learning, Understanding Students, Adding to Your Repertoire of Skills and Strategies for Facilitating Active Learning, Teaching for Higher Level Goals, and Lifelong Learning for the Teacher. While McKeachie overall does an excellent job, most of the focus is on teaching traditional aged college students.

The Authors

Michael Brady began teaching in 1977 at a community college in Connecticut. In 1984, he and his family moved to Maine where be became professor of adult education at the University of Southern Maine. His courses involve a wide range of subjects including the history and philosophy of adult education, action research, gerontology, death and dying, and the facilitation of adult learning. In addition, every summer he facilitates a travel course entitled "Baseball and American Society: A Journey," which won a national higher education award. Mike also serves as Senior Research Fellow in the Osher Lifelong Learning Institute, a "Senior College" at the University of Southern Maine designed for learners age 50 and older. His three previous books are entitled *Perspectives on Adult Learning, Retirement: The Challenge of Change,* and *The Spirit of Teaching.* Mike and his wife of 25 years, Nancy, live in Gorham, Maine. They have three adult children—Ryan, Meghan, and Maura.

Mike has degrees from St. Mary's Seminary and University (B.A., M.Div.) and the University of Connecticut (M.S.W., Ph.D.)

Allen Lampert loves to teach. After a distinguished 13-year career in banking culminating as bank president in Boston, Allen entered his first adult education classroom in Wells, Maine, in 1995 and has not left it since. He now spends his time as an adult education teacher working for Portland Public Schools teaching courses in Business English, Keyboarding, Office Communication, and a variety of job training programs. He also works as an adjunct faculty member for the University of Southern Maine's Adult Education Department teaching a graduate seminar on transformation learning theory. In his spare time, he conducts teaching workshops and has co-authored *Understanding What You Read.* Allen and his wife, Leslie, live in Old Orchard Beach, Maine with their two sons, Benjamin and Samuel.

Allen has degrees from the University of California, Berkeley (B.A.) and the University of Southern Maine (M.S.).

The Spirit of Teaching

Edited by
E. Michael Brady *and* **Desi Larson**

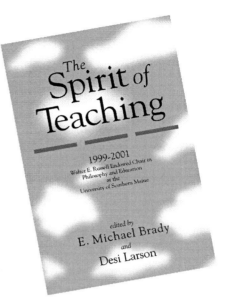

Table of Contents

ANNOUNCEMENTS & EVENTS

WMO Giving - Please prayerfully consider giving a special gift to our World Mission Offering this Easter season!

Summer Schedule of Events - Please pick up a Summer Events brochure from around the church to stay up-to-date on all upcoming events!

Spring Library Giveaway - Stop by the FBC Library and guess how many jelly beans are in the jar for a chance to win one of our many prizes (including candy, CDs, books, and more)!

Senior Recognition Sunday is May 19! If you are a senior in high school, please be sure to register for this and the Senior Banquet on our website by April 21. See Jon Kyle for more information (jallred@fbcmurray.org).

Kids Camp Scholarships - Our Kids1st 2nd-5th graders are headed to Crossings this summer! We want every child who desires to go to be able to attend. To do that, we need YOUR help! We are in need of 3 Kids Camp scholarships at $310 each. If you can help sponsor all or part of a scholarship, please put your gift in the offering plate or bring it to the church office and designate "Kids Camp Scholarship."

Fellowship Supper Menu this week is meatloaf, hashbrown casserole, corn, salad, rolls, dessert.

MidWeek - Three new adult MidWeek studies began recently. It's not too late to sign up for your study of choice on the sign-up sheets in the Welcome Center, by calling the church office (270-753-1854), or on our website under "Get Involved."

Baby Dedication - This year's Baby Dedication is on Mother's Day, May 12. If you would like to dedicate your child, please sign up on our website or email Rachel (rriquelme@fbcmurray.org). There will be a one-time class during the Sunday School hour on May 5 in room 301 to prepare and instruct parents.

THIS WEEK AT FBC

Sunday, April 21, 2019
Worship Service	8:30 am
Sunday School	9:45 am
Worship Service	11:00 am

No Evening Activities

Monday, April 22
M.A.G.I.C. Potluck	12:00 pm

Tuesday, April 23
Breakfast Club @ Murray Donuts (Students)	6:45 am
Mother's Day Out	8:30 am

Wednesday, April 24
Mother's Day Out	8:30 am
Prayer Meeting	12:00 pm
Fellowship Supper	5:15 pm
MSM Fusion (Students)	5:45 pm
KidsFirst MidWeek	6:15 pm
MidWeek (Adults)	6:15 pm
HSM Awaken (Students)	6:30 pm

Thursday, April 25
Mother's Day Out	8:30 am

2019 GIVING

$ 25,977.20	Budget Receipts from 04/14/2019
$ 378,135.00	Budgeted YTD
$ 354,810.61	Budget Receipts YTD
$ 1,760.80	WMO Receipts from 04/14/2019
$ 140,000.00	WMO 2019 Goal
$ 21,402.69	WMO Receipts YTD
$ 19,581.00	FLC Receipts from 04/14/2019
$ 2,336,281.29	FLC Receipts to Date
$ 1,457,159.88	FLC Borrowed to Date

Order Form

To order *The New Teacher of Adults* or *The Spirit of Teaching*, fill out and submit this form.

First Name:_____Last Name: _____

Title: _____

Address:_____

City: _____State:_____Zip: _____

Phone: _____E-mail Address: _____

Method of payment: ❑ Payment Enclosed   ❑ Bill me (Net 30 days)
Please make check or money order payable to *New Teacher Concepts*.

❑ *The New Teacher of Adults* ($16.95 each)
                    Number of Copies:____ x $16.95 = $_____
❑ *The Spirit of Teaching* ($9.95 each)
                    Number of Copies:____ x $9.95 = $_____

          ME Sales Tax (5%), if applicable = $_____

      Shipping/Handling (Refer to chart below) = $_____

                          Total Due = $_____

New Teacher Concepts
6 Ridgewood Drive
Old Orchard Beach, ME 04064

Allen Lampert: alamper1@maine.rr.com
Michael Brady: mbrady@usm.maine.edu

Phone: (207) 934-4299
FAX: (207) 775-0616

www.newteacherconcepts.com

Shipping/Handling Chart

Purchase	S/H Cost
1-2 books	$5.95 minimum
$59.99 or less	Add 15% of total cost
$60-$99.99	Add 13%
$100-$299.99	Add 10%
$300-$499.99	Add 8%
over $500	Add 7%

*International orders may be subject to additional shipping charges.